Awesome Women On The Move

Inspirational

Affirmations | Scriptures | Quotes

TENARIA DRUMMOND-SMITH
With 30 CO-AUTHOR WOMEN

Awesome Women On The Move
INSPIRATIONAL Daily Journal
Copyright ©2019 by Tenaria Drummond-Smith

All rights reserved. No part of this book may be reproduced, copied, stored or transmitted in any form or by any means – graphic, electronic, or mechanical, including photocopying, recording, or information storage and retrieval systems without the prior written permission of Tenaria Drummond-Smith or HOV Publishing except where permitted by law.

Unless otherwise noted, Scripture is taken from the King James Version. Copyright © 1982 by Thomas Nelson, Inc. Used by permission. All rights reserved.

Scripture taken from the New King James Version®. Copyright © 1982 by Thomas Nelson. Used by permission. All rights reserved.

Holy Bible, New Living Translation, copyright © 1996, 2004, 2015 by Tyndale House Foundation. Used by permission of Tyndale House Publishers, Inc., Carol Stream, Illinois 60188. All rights reserved.

Holy Bible, New International Version®, NIV® Copyright ©1973, 1978, 1984, 2011 by Biblica, Inc.® Used by permission. All rights reserved worldwide.

Amplified Bible (AMP) Copyright © 2015 by The Lockman Foundation, La Habra, CA 90631. All rights reserved.

The Message (MSG)
Copyright © 1993, 2002, 2018 by Eugene H. Peterson

The Holy Bible, English Standard Version. ESV® Text Edition: 2016. Copyright © 2001 by Crossway Bibles, a publishing ministry of Good News Publishers.

HOV Publishing a division of HOV, LLC.
www.hovpub.com / hopeofvision@gmail.com

Cover Design: HOV Design Solutions
Editor/Proofreader: Jeff Smith and HOV Publishing

Write the author Tenaria Drummond-Smith at: tds@awesomewomenonthemove.org
For more information about special discounts for bulk purchases,
please contact Tenaria Drummond-Smith or hopeofvision@gmail.com

Paperback ISBN: 978-1-942871-67-5
eBook ISBN: 978-1-942871-68-2
Library of Congress Control Number:

10 9 8 7 6 5 4 3 2

Printed in the United States of America

ABOUT THE

Inspirational Daily Journal

Tenaria Drummond-Smith, founder and visionary of Awesome Women On The Move. I was inspired to do an Inspirational Journal because I wanted women from different walks of life to write from their hearts so that readers could glean from their experiences. If we could put a smile on someone's face, then we know that this isn't just another journal. As an encouraging collection of Affirmations, Scriptures, and Quotes, we want this book to have a positive impact on lives. Start your day with real words from real people.

MEET THE 31 CO-AUTHORS

Tenaria Drummond-Smith I Jacquelene Scruggs I Sophia L. Greene I Theresa Byrd I Vera Moore I Leslie Duroseau I Linda M. Johnson I Dawn M. Coles I Kendra Renee' Manigault I Latricia T. Davis I Cherryl Simpson I Jean Thompson I Antionette Halsey I Tiffany D. Kelly I Nina D. Brown I Keeva Dedewo I Dawn Grantham I Roberta Jones-Johnson I Bernetta Green I Debra D. Carter I Karen M. Carter I Sherell Ferrer I Rosemary Hart I Deborah Perry I Kimberly Bailey I Miranda Rivers I Esther Burgess I Jessie Striggles I Alicia Bailey I Jae (Joyce) Rollins I Treinna Thomas

@AwesomeWomenOnTheMove
e: tds@awesomewomenonthemove.org

Awesome Women On The Move

Inspirational

Affirmations | Scriptures | Quotes

Inspirational Affirmation

ENTRY BY: TENARIA DRUMMOND-SMITH

DAY 1

God has made each and EVERY one of us differently and to be what He created us to be. His word clearly exemplifies who we are, and we're not to question it. Some want to look or act like other people This tells me that they're not looking into their own selves to find their inner beauty. Not every one of us is going to be thin, fat, light-skinned, dark-skinned, long-haired, short-haired, or with no hair. Some might have straight teeth, crooked teeth, or no teeth. Does that change the fact of what God says about us? Sometimes, wanting to be or look like another will make you lose focus on who you really are. Are you that person who can give a compliment to another person? Are you that person who knows how to celebrate another who's being awarded? Let the word of God resonate in your mind and heart and help you become a better "you."

"I will praise thee; for I am fearfully and wonderfully made: marvellous are thy works; and that my soul knoweth right well."

—Psalm 139:14

Inspirational Scripture

ENTRY BY: JACQUELENE SCRUGGS

DAY *2*

When I think of the goodness of Jesus and all that He has done for me, I apply this scripture:

"O give thanks unto the LORD; for he is good: for his mercy endureth for ever."

—Psalm136:1

Inspirational Affirmation

ENTRY BY: SOPHIA L. GREENE

DAY *3*

As I rise to face this day, I greet this present situation as the only way to give of myself, sharing the best that I can possibly share with the world. I take charge of my thoughts and intentionally walk with the authority of my presence to step wherever there is darkness and add more light —stepping out of Babylon one step at a time.

Inspirational Affirmation

ENTRY BY: THERESA BYRD

DAY *4*

SERENITY PRAYER

God grant me the serenity
To accept the things I cannot change;
Courage to change the things I can;
And wisdom to know the difference.

Living one day at a time;
Enjoying one moment at a time;
Accepting hardships as the pathway to peace;
Taking, as He did, this sinful world
As it is, not as I would have it;
Trusting that He will make all things right
If I surrender to His Will;
So that I may be reasonably happy in this life
And supremely happy with Him
Forever and ever in the next.
Amen.

—Reinhold Niebuhr

Inspirational Scripture

ENTRY BY: VERA MOORE

DAY *5*

"[1]The LORD is my shepherd; I shall not want."
"[4]Yea, though I walk through the valley of the shadow of death, I will fear no evil: for thou art with me; thy rod and thy staff they comfort me."

—Psalm 23:1,4

These are some of the first scriptures most of us learn as children. However, when you really understand and accept Christ for yourselves, you are not just reading them as children being taught a Sunday school verse. You're understanding the depth and significance of this passage. A shepherd takes care of his flock. He will go after the "one": (YOU)!

Have you ever really stopped, just for a moment, and thought about how God protects us? Have you ever stopped and thought about how close your shadow is? Next time see if you can separate yourself from your shadow.

Let me know! (vmoore@veramoorecosmetics.com)

Inspirational Scripture

ENTRY BY: LESLIE DUROSEAU

DAY *6*

"Before I formed you in the womb I knew you [and approved of you as My chosen instrument], And before you were born I consecrated you [to Myself as My own]; I have appointed you as a prophet to the nations."

—Jeremiah 1:5 (AMP)

Inspirational Affirmation

ENTRY BY: LINDA M. JOHNSON

DAY *7*

A RENEWED MIND

God is love. His love cannot be compared to anything on this earth because it is eternal. A renewed mind will allow you to think positive. A positive attitude will get you through every situation.

"Finally, brethren, whatsoever things are true, whatsoever things are honest, whatsoever things are just, whatsoever things are pure, whatsoever things are lovely, whatsoever things are of good report; if there be any virtue, and if there be any praise, think on these things."

—Philippians 4:8

Positive Thinking Will Make You Happy

Inspirational Affirmation

ENTRY BY: DAWN M. COLES

DAY *8*

MY CUP RUNS OVER

"You prepare a table before me in the presence of my enemies; You anoint my head with oil; My cup runs over."

—Psalm 23:5 (NKJV)

This scripture is such an inspiration, especially in those times when you feel things are closing in and you're pushed almost beyond your own strength and endurance. When I think of the cup, I think of how it represents our normal portion in life according to what God gives each person as he pleases.

I imagine this cup running over from the cares and responsibilities of life, but the psalmist states that God has prepared a table for him (and us). God, the one who created, molded, and shaped us, our Father who knows all about us, has taken the time to prepare a table for us. I envision a table with the finest china. My cup is made of porcelain that has been through the fire. He, the creator of the heavens and earth, has anointed us with oil that's represented by the Holy Spirit and has provided all that we will ever need, even in times when our portion in life is crushing us. This should change our perspective towards the cup, so instead of seeing it overflowing with weakness and being half empty, see our cup as overflowing with strength from on high. Thank you, Holy Spirit, my cup runs over.

Inspirational Affirmation

ENTRY BY: KENDRA RENEE' MANIGAULT

DAY *9*

I'm Confident!

"Thank You for making me so wonderfully complex! Your workmanship is marvelous —how well I know it."

—Psalm 139:14 (NLT)

Inspirational Scripture

ENTRY BY: LATRICIA T. DAVIS

DAY *10*

LOVE IS

"For God so loved the world, that he gave his only begotten Son, that whosoever believeth in him should not perish, but have everlasting life."

—John 3:16

I had it all wrong when It came to understanding what "REAL LOVE" was and what it felt like. I thought for a very long time that love was based on what a person could do for you, or the tangible and material items they gave you. I thought those things were of value, only to find out later in my life that I was wrong. Many have tried to define the true meaning and essence of the word "LOVE," only to fail at it.

I was young and naive when it came to expressing and receiving love to the point that I found myself in a relationship filled with nothing but violence. I thought love was supposed to be this way because every time I was verbally and physically abused, my abuser would say, "I love you" afterwards. Still feeling the pain and bearing the scars of my nightmare, I wanted to end it all forever. I had to find a way to go on and live not just for my children, but for myself. I once heard a preacher say, "When you have problems in your life that you can't seem to solve, talk to God about it, and find the answer to your problem in the Bible." I was at a point in my life where I felt that no one cared. I only knew the love of my children, and my abuser, until I received Jesus Christ as my Savior. I began to read the Bible, and in it, I found the source of my strength in every word that I read. This form of love is called "AGAPE LOVE." God's love, at the end of the day, is all that matters and will last forever. He's patient, kind, and faithful. His love never fails, and never runs out. Love yourself and find your true "LOVE" in God, not in man or materials things that come and go. Remember that you are so loved by God.

Inspirational Scripture

ENTRY BY: CHERRYL SIMPSON

DAY *11*

"You will keep in [a]perfect and constant peace the one whose mind is steadfast [that is, committed and focused on You—in both [b]inclination and character], Because he trusts and takes refuge in You [with hope and confident expectation]."

—Isaiah 26:3 (AMP)

As children of the most high God, we often go through challenges that may cause us to fear, or to question our faith or even our belief system. We may feel the lack of peace due to these challenges but understanding and soon over-standing that these trials or challenges are merely there to strengthen us. We will soon change our perspective on each of them as we depend on our Heavenly Father during each episode.

As a young woman, I absolutely hated the idea of going through hardship; it just was so scary for me. Perhaps, I was never taught how to deal with a crisis, even though as a nurse, I was in the mode of teaching and encouraging families through their trials. It seemed so easy to encourage or build up another person, because I was outside that picture frame. As for my challenges, it was frightening, and I didn't feel good about them at all, until one day I asked the Lord to help me see what He sees, and to get through whatever it is that I need to get through. Things didn't become easier after that, but I knew He had me in the palm of His hand. After spending time in His word, I felt a peace, and I could rest in what He said to me because I keep my mind/heart on Him. His promises will never fail me!

Inspirational Affirmation

ENTRY BY: JEAN THOMPSON

DAY *12*

LORD, I CALLED

Lord, Lord, I called on you this morning to say I am awake.
Lord, I called to say it's me, your child.
Lord, did you get my call?

I just wanted to say I thank you for watching over me last night.
I thank you for the strength to rise early this morning. To be able to clothe myself and bend down to lace up my shoes.
Lord, you are awesome and amazing.
You're so worthy to be praised.

I'm grateful to have awakened from my bed of comfort and not from the cold sidewalk of stone, or in some homeless shelter, as I remember from years ago.
Lord, you have been so good to me, and I cannot tell it all today.

So, I will call on you again tomorrow, and the next day.
Expressing my gratitude and thanks for all that you have done for me and will do.

May the God of hope fill you with joy and peace (Romans 15:13).

Inspirational Scripture

ENTRY BY: ANTOINETTE HALSEY

DAY *13*

"And blessed is she that believed: for there shall be a performance of those things which were told her from the Lord."

—Luke 1:45

Inspirational Quote

ENTRY BY: TIFFANY D. KELLY

DAY *14*

I am built for success! Nothing can stop me from greatness but me. I am capable of making decisions for a successful future.

—Tiffany D. Kelly

Inspirational Affirmation

ENTRY BY: NINA D. BROWN

DAY *15*

THE SILENT FIGHT (Galatians 2:20)

You prepared for this. You sacrificed for this, you cried for this and lost so much for this. You made some hard choices for this, as this has cost you everything.

Focus, you say. How? when I cannot drown out the chants of the people who remind me of my past? How? when they are shouting the truth of my failures and putting my past on public display? How can I focus when they are shouting the secrets to my truth? As the stench of defeat clogs my nostrils and overwhelms me with the sense of defeat, my hope is lost as failure presents itself as my portion.

Then He whispers, "Remember the promise before the journey. On that journey, you found trust, love, hope, and perseverance. And on this journey, you found, faith, courage, confidence, and strength to keep going when quitting would have been your right to take."

He wipes your face and whispers again, "The fights were all fixed". This small insignificant moment in time is just that, a moment in time, and in 60 seconds it will be gone. Remember, faith kept you, guided you, and has given you the fortitude to continue when you were unsure of the end. You're in the last round. Look around, you've been here before, and despite the scorecard, you can still come out on top. See my beloved, this round counts the most. Remember the journey. I will never leave you nor forsake you."

The bell rings as the crowds jump to its feet. You duck and swerve, you shift your weight and take the final punches, and then everything goes BLACK...ding, ding, ding, the referee takes your arm and declares you the winner by KO!

Inspirational Affirmation

ENTRY BY: KEEVA DEDEWO

DAY *16*

I AM DESTINED FOR

GREATNESS

—KEEVA DEDEWO

Inspirational Affirmation

ENTRY BY: DAWN GRANTHAM

DAY *17*

Praises go up, and blessings come down

When life is turned upside down, humble yourselves, and praise God, because the enemy is on his job to kill, steal, and destroy, but fear not; God is positioning you to prosper.

Inspirational Affirmation

ENTRY BY: ROBERTA JONES-JOHNSON

DAY *18*

P-U-S-H
Persevere Until Something Happens

Inspirational Quote

ENTRY BY: BERNETTA GREEN

DAY *19*

Dishonest scales are an abomination unto the Lord, but a just weight is His delight. With pride comes shame, but with humility there is wisdom, and the integrity of the upright will deliver them (based on Proverbs 11:1-3 NKJV).

Inspirational Scripture

ENTRY BY: DEBRA D. CARTER

DAY *20*

"Lift up my eyes to the mountains—where does my help come from? My help comes from the Lord, the Maker of heaven and earth. He will not let your foot slip—he who watches over you will not slumber; indeed, he who watches over Israel will neither slumber nor sleep."

—Psalm 121:1-4 (NIV)

Inspirational Quote

ENTRY BY: KAREN M. CARTER

DAY *21*

"Put one foot in front of the other and do your walk!"
(As told to me by my mother, Narrie Carter)

My mom possessed a tremendous amount of wisdom and common sense. While I was growing up, she shared encouraging words of faith and love with me. She was my best teacher, supporter, and friend. I recall how as a little girl, I would watch her leaving the house to go to work, admiring her proud carriage as she walked out the door with such beauty, dignity, and strength.

In her nineties, Mom walked with limited mobility, using a cane for support. We often strolled together around Argyle Lake and one evening, after a short distance, Mom stopped and said, "I used to be able to walk, but YOU, you put one foot in front of the other and do your walk!" As if she passed the baton, I continued my walk and placed those words deep within my spirit, knowing that one day, I would need to recall them. I lost Mom that following year; she was just shy of her ninety-third birthday. Despite my hurt, disappointment, and pain, those words re-surfaced, encouraging me to press forward. I continue walking through life with faith, courage, strength, victory, truth, and love, feeling extremely blessed to have had her as my Mom!

Inspirational Scripture

ENTRY BY: SHERELL FERRER

DAY *22*

"(For we walk by faith, not by sight:)"

—2 Corinthians 5:7

FAITH

On October 3rd, 1998, my husband and I said "I do" to each other before family and friends. After the ceremony and reception were over, it was now time to deal with reality. We had no clue where we would reside, but we were certain that God had us covered. We went on our week-long honeymoon and upon returning, my parents announced that they purchased a home and would be moving out. Just like that, God provided for us because we put our faith and trust in him alone.

Inspirational Affirmation

ENTRY BY: ROSEMARY HART

DAY *23*

Transcending barriers...

by persevering and moving forward. Reading positive-thinking books (i.e. Bible, Think & Grow Rich, etc.) is key to your growth.

—Rosemary Hart

Inspirational Scripture

ENTRY BY: DEBORAH PERRY

DAY *24*

"Who can find a virtuous woman? for her price is far above rubies."

—Proverbs 31:10

Proverbs 31 speaks of a virtuous woman. When my mother raised me, she raised to be that virtuous woman. A woman that God would find available to use, and that a man would find delightful to be his wife and choose to be the mother of his children.

Always be the woman HE is looking for.

Inspirational Quote

ENTRY BY: KIMBERLY BAILEY

DAY *25*

"Never lose your faith, always have hope."

—C. Berkeley

Inspirational Quote

ENTRY BY: MIRANDA RIVERS

DAY *26*

"I have peace of mind only when I forgive rather than judge."

"Once we forgive others for wronging us, we start to forgive ourselves."

—Gerald Jampolsky

"Judge not, and you shall not be judged; Condemn not, and you shall not be condemned. Forgive, and you will be forgiven."

—Luke 6:37 (NKJV)

Inspirational Scripture

ENTRY BY: ESTHER BURGESS

DAY *27*

"The steps of a good man are ordered by the LORD: and he delighteth in his way."

—Psalm 37:23

"Unless thy law had been my delights, I should then have perished in mine affliction."

—Psalm 119:92

Inspirational Scripture

ENTRY BY: JESSIE STRIGGLES

DAY *28*

"Every man according as he purposeth in his heart, so let him give; not grudgingly, or of necessity: for God loveth a cheerful giver."

—2 Corinthians 9:7

GOD LOVETH A CHEERFUL GIVER!!!!

There was a time that I didn't know that was scripture; it was just my heart to give. I never knew a lack of money.

EVERYTHING I TOUCHED CREATED MORE MONEY FOR ME.

Inspirational Scripture

ENTRY BY: ALICIA BAILEY

DAY *29*

"Trust in the LORD with all thine heart; and lean not unto thine own understanding. In all thy ways acknowledge him, and he shall direct thy paths."

—Proverbs 3:5-6

Proverbs 3:5-6 is my favorite scriptural reference. As I get older, I realize that I must be determined to put all of my trust and hope in God. There have been times in my life where I have made decisions without consulting God first. However, I thank God that one day, my mind was transformed and my eyes were opened to the things of God.

We are living in a world where we cannot afford to believe that we can live an abundant life without allowing God to direct our paths. When we allow God to lead us, we will reach our full potential and destiny in Him. When we make a conscious decision to listen to the voice of God, we will be able to overcome any challenge that arises in our life. When we allow God to be the Author and Finisher of our faith, He will keep us from falling.

Today, I am declaring that my God is Awesome! My God is able to supply my needs and your needs. My God is a True Shepherd, and He is a Healer! My God is able to move mountains. My God will protect you! When we stay focused on God and acknowledge Him for who He is, we will live a more joyous life! The best advice I can give to anyone who needs guidance is to trust God.

Inspirational Quote

ENTRY BY: JAE (JOYCE) ROLLINS

DAY *30*

Many Christians grow up in church,
but never grow in Christ.
They know hymns,
But they don't know "HIM."

—Unknown

Inspirational Quote

ENTRY BY: TREINNA THOMAS

DAY *31*

DARE TO BE DIFFERENT.
THERE'S ONLY ONE OF YOU!

—Treinna Thomas

Inspirational Affirmation

ENTRY BY: TENARIA DRUMMOND-SMITH

DAY *32*

Are you someone who comes from a family that had very little education and money? Today is a new day to break that cycle. You will go to school to get a high school diploma or graduate from college. This doesn't have to be you anymore. You have to make up in your mind that you want better for yourself. You don't have to look like what you've been through. Be that living testimony. God is clear in His word that we're able to defeat those things that have us bound. We know that we're more than conquerors through Him. Be encouraged and make that first step for change.

"Nay, in all these things we are more than conquerors through him that loved us."

—Romans 8:37

Inspirational Scripture

ENTRY BY: JACQUELENE SCRUGGS

DAY *33*

When the devil attacks you in your body, your mind, your finances and your family, trust the word of God that says,

"I will bless the LORD at all times: his praise shall continually be in my mouth."

—Psalm 34:1

Inspirational Affirmation

ENTRY BY: SOPHIA L. GREENE

DAY *34*

Today, I choose to have a board meeting face to face with all these wonderful, loyal servants. Even when I am asleep, they have served me —without complaint— with such love and honor. I thank them individually and collectively as the greatest team in my life. Today, I choose to extend gratitude and love to my body and all my organs for being so faithful for over five decades. Honoring my body is honoring Jah.

Inspirational Quote

ENTRY BY: THERESA BYRD

DAY *35*

All of my good days
Out-weigh my bad days
I won't complain

—"I Won't Complain", by Reverend Paul Jones

Inspirational Scripture

ENTRY BY: VERA MOORE

DAY *36*

1Children, obey your parents in the Lord: for this is right. 2Honor thy father and mother; which is the first commandment with promise;

11Put on the whole armour of God, that ye may be able to stand against the wiles of the devil. 12For we wrestle not against flesh and blood, but against principalities, against powers, against the rulers of the darkness of this world, against spiritual wickedness in high places.

—Ephesians 6:1-2, 11-12

Sound familiar?

In the natural world, no one can go to battle without the proper armor. It's evident we are dealing with something bigger than ourselves. We are dealing with spiritual warfare! Read Ephesians, and you will not be shocked at the times that we are living in! However, "...be strong in the Lord, and in the power of his might." (Ephesian 6:10) The only way I have made it through these past forty years is in knowing that God was watching my blindside. I have a Protector, a Provider, and a Comforter who will never leave or forsake me. That's a WOW!

Inspirational Affirmation

ENTRY BY: LESLIE DUROSEAU

DAY *37*

Independence: Your Freedom Begins With You

FAWOHODIE is the Adrinka symbol that reminds us that it is our divine right to be free, to be independent. What does that mean? It means to be authentically you. The "you" that was created in the image of God; the image of the divine.

For many years I believed the lies that were either directly or indirectly told to me about me. Whether it was television shows with their disparaging images of black people, or how the greater society and community reacted to me, or failed to respond to me. I often grew up wanting to be something other than what I was —a brown girl living in America. Dreams deferred, my identity in crisis, and torn between what I knew, what I was being told, and whether it even mattered at all.

One day when I was in my twenties and feeling overwhelmed with life, I lifted up my head, uncertain to whom or what I was speaking to, and asked; "Is this what I was created for? To endure suffering, hardship, and struggle?" And just like that, I heard a voice say, "NO my daughter. I created you for so much more. Come out from under the lies. For I know you, I formed you. You are destined for so much more. Greatness lies within you."

It is from that day forth that I decided I wanted to be free. No longer bound by what others say, think or even what they would try to do to me. I took a leap of faith. I promised myself and the God that I serve that I will go forth, and I am willing to die doing it. My freedom means that I don't have all the answers, I don't have all the directions, or all the instructions. What I do know is that all I need resides within me. For I am wonderfully and fearfully made. Created in the "*imago Dei*", the image of God.

Inspirational Affirmation

ENTRY BY: LINDA M. JOHNSON

DAY *38*

DO NOT WORRY

Live your life to your fullest potential. For if you believe, you will receive whatever you ask God for in prayer.

"But seek ye first the kingdom of God, and his righteousness; and all these things shall be added unto you."

—Matthew 6:33

Positive Thinking Will Make You Happy

Inspirational Affirmation

ENTRY BY: DAWN M. COLES

DAY *39*

CARRIERS OF PEACE

6Be anxious for nothing, but in everything by prayer and
supplication, with thanksgiving, let your requests be made known
to God; 7and the peace of God, which surpasses all
understanding, will guard your hearts and minds through
Christ Jesus."

—Philippians 4:6-7 (NKJV)

The Lord promises us peace, which is a fruit of the spirit that I value and must dwell in daily. Peace is priceless. I will not allow my personal peace, whether in my household, the workplace, or relationships, to be compromised. The word of God states we should not be anxious about anything. There are times this may seem difficult to do, but then prayer and petitioning God come into place. When I seek him in prayer, his peace comes upon me in my situations.

Webster defines peace as "a quiet and calm state of mind, a place of agreement and harmony". In this place, I have clarity of thought. I can make a wise decision, and my emotions are under control. Clutter is removed; I have a bird's eye view of things. I can be an efficient and effective communicator, moving and operating in peace. There was a bumper sticker on cars that said, "No Jesus, No Peace. Know Jesus, Know Peace". When I dwell in peace, this becomes my reality because I know Jesus, I know and carry peace. The peace of the Lord transcends all understanding. This is the peace we must extend to others. The world is looking for peace and we are ambassadors for Christ. We must carry the peace of God, so I encourage you to walk in PEACE.

Inspirational Scripture

ENTRY BY: KENDRA RENEE' MANIGAULT

DAY *40*

Focused, Forward, & Finish!

"I press toward the mark for the prize of the high calling of God in Christ Jesus."

—Philippians 3:14

Inspirational Scripture

ENTRY BY: LATRICIA T. DAVIS

DAY *41*

PRAISE HIM

"I will bless the LORD at all times: his praise shall continually be in my mouth."

—Psalm 34:1

Praise is what I do every day when I wake up and realize that God has blessed me with another day, and another opportunity to live. It was my praises unto God that brought me through some of the darkest and difficult moments in my life. Throughout my lifetime, I have learned that, no matter what I'm going through, to continue to praise God. We are commanded in the scriptures to praise God because of the things that He does for us. He provides all of our "NEEDS," and even some of our "WANTS." That's the kind of God He is, even when we don't deserve things. He's faithful.

I've discovered that my praise is a weapon of warfare, and like a trumpet, the sound that resonates from it pierces the very heart of God. He is moved with compassion to act on my behalf, simply because He loves and cares for you and me. I make it a habit every day when I wake up to give God praise and thanks for my life. Good, bad, or indifferent, God is still worthy to be praised. Let the praises of God continuously be in your mouth. Put on your garment of praise.

My prayer: Lord I thank you for all you've done for me. I thank you for providing for me, for keeping me, loving me, and most importantly, I thank you for the breath in my body to bless and praise you with my mouth continuously. Amen.

Inspirational Scripture

ENTRY BY: CHERRYL SIMPSON

DAY *42*

"And be not conformed to this world: but be ye transformed by the renewing of your mind, that ye may prove what is that good, and acceptable, and perfect, will of God."

—Romans 12:2

As we continue on our journey, we attempt to draw near to God every day. We desire and say that He is our source and this is a fact, whether we realize it or not. The world has all kinds of similar perspectives on who God is and how He wants us to live. People will use His name and quote passages from the Bible, but let me tell you something, if He's not there where you are going, then go another way. It's important to read the Word of God every day and to meditate on it, too. Spending time with Him and talking with Him daily will help us as we grow in understanding who He really is.

The Bible will help you as you grow in your faith, and what's even more significant is how the Holy Spirit will show you exactly what you need to do for every circumstance. He is our compass and our guide. He directs, He teaches, and He leads us into all truth. He knows exactly what we are going through, and specifically knows how to help us. As we renew our minds by reading and ingesting His word, we become more sensitive to the Holy Spirit, and the choices we make will certainly change. The old program of our mind needs a new download, and once we over-stand this, we will live better lives, we will make better choices, and we will see His manifestations come alive right before our eyes.

Inspirational Scripture

ENTRY BY: JEAN THOMPSON

DAY *43*

HEALING

"[14]If my people, which are called by my name, shall humble themselves, and pray, and seek my face, and turn from their wicked ways; then will I hear from heaven, and will forgive their sin, and will heal their land. [15]Now mine eyes shall be open, and mine ears attent unto the prayer that is made in this place."

—2 Chronicles 7:14-15

Inspirational Scripture

ENTRY BY: ANTOINETTE HALSEY

DAY *44*

"And we know that all things work together for good to them that love God, to them who are the called according to his purpose."

—Romans 8:28

Inspirational Quote

ENTRY BY: TIFFANY D. KELLY

DAY *45*

Think about a challenge you thought you couldn't overcome, but God brought you that. So what makes you think God won't bring you through this challenge too? Stand in your POWER and push past your challenges. God got you!

—Tiffany D. Kelly

Inspirational Affirmation

ENTRY BY: NINA D. BROWN

DAY *46*

EXCUSE ME, CAN YOU DIRECT ME TO MY SEAT?

"Freedom is when you can sit with the hurt of your past with no regrets loving, and no regrets of leaving."

Excuse me, can you direct me to my seat? The maître d says, "Sure, give me a moment. May I see your invitation?"

This room is nothing you have ever seen before, and everything is in place. The maître d returns your invitation and apologizes for the wait. He says, "Give me a few moments and I will take you to your table." Hmm, these faces look familiar. You check your invitation and the information is correct.

You are early. Yes, that's unusual. You walk towards the sea of tables where Ms. Rejection and Mr. Loneliness are sitting with Ms. Depression and Lady Suicide. Clearly, this invitation must be wrong. We pass Sir Anger and his wife, Lady Revenge. Then there is a familiar laugh. You turn to see the triplets Liar, Stealer, and Killer, with Mr. Brokenness, Ms. Bitter, Mr. Adulterer, Ms. Insecure, Mr. Arrogant, and Dr. Jealousy with his wife, Mrs. Envy. This is really a bad joke gone wrong.

There clearly must be a mistake because what is this crowd doing here? Just as you were prepared to ask the question, the maître d says, "Here is your seat." You look up and see you're at the front of the room. Your name is on the place setting as the maître d apologizes again for not knowing your time of arrival. See, the guest of honor is never too early for their own party. The maître d pulls your seat out and welcomes you to your celebration and says, "I hope you'll enjoy yourself, with no regrets of attending." See, this guest list is what you've overcome. You have the best seat in the house.

Inspirational Scripture

ENTRY BY: KEEVA DEDEWO

DAY *47*

"[12]I know what it is to be in need, and I know what it is to have plenty. I have learned the secret of being content in any and every situation, whether well fed or hungry, whether living in plenty or in want. [13]I can do everything through him who gives me strength."

—Philippians 4:12-13 (NIV)

Inspirational Scripture

ENTRY BY: DAWN GRANTHAM

DAY 48

"Beloved, I wish above all things that thou mayest prosper and be in health, even as thy soul prospereth."

—3 John 1:2

Inspirational Affirmation

ENTRY BY: ROBERTA JONES-JOHNSON

DAY *49*

Life is like a ballgame: the next play is coming.
You may not know when or from where, but it's coming…
BE READY!!!

—Roberta Jones-Johnson

Inspirational Affirmation

ENTRY BY: BERNETTA GREEN

DAY *50*

EXPRESSION

I am blessed in numerous ways, and good health is a place to call my home. Communication with my family and my Creator has placed me just where I need to be to focus on myself, and all positive and productive things about myself. I have many complexities within me that I must live with, deal with, and it is a necessity that I personally assess them by keeping in mind that my Creator is the only just judge.

Inspirational Scripture

ENTRY BY: DEBRA D. CARTER

DAY *51*

"but those who hope in the Lord will renew their strength. They will soar on wings like eagles; they will run and not grow weary, they will walk and not be faint."

—Isaiah 40:31 (NIV)

Inspirational Scripture

ENTRY BY: KAREN M. CARTER

DAY *52*

"[13]...But one thing I do: Forgetting what is behind and straining toward what is ahead, [14]I press on toward the goal to win the prize for which God has called me heavenward in Christ Jesus."

—Philippians 3:13-14 (NIV)

Inspirational Scripture

ENTRY BY: SHERELL FERRER

DAY 53

"He said to her, 'Daughter, your faith has healed you. Go in peace and be freed from your suffering.'"

—Mark 5:34 (NIV)

HEALING

On February 14th, 2011, I was supposed to have minor surgery to remove a cyst from my throat. I was released the following day because no complications occurred. When I reached my mother's house, I begin to have difficulty breathing. I started gasping for air, fell to the floor and crawled, searching for air. My mom was on the phone with the 911 operator, steadily pleading the blood of Jesus. My little brother decided the ambulance was taking too long to come, so he rushed me to the hospital in his car.

I was taken to the emergency room for immediate care and doctors were astonished. They said I made it just in time because my airways were so swollen that they were about to close up. I was placed in a medically induced coma for seven days. When I awakened, I was hooked up to a breathing tube, but I was able to write. I told my husband to take a picture…a testimony. Even on my sick bed, I trusted God to heal me completely and he did just that.

Inspirational Quote

ENTRY BY: ROSEMARY HART

DAY *54*

Discipline...staying focused...keep your eyes on your goals and employ discipline to stick with it! Surround yourself with like-minded people.

—Rosemary Hart

Inspirational Scripture

ENTRY BY: DEBORAH PERRY

DAY *55*

"For I know the thoughts that I think toward you, saith the Lord, thoughts of peace, and not of evil, to give you an expected end."

—Jeremiah 29:11

The scripture in Jeremiah speaks of His thoughts and plans. When I hear this scripture, it reminds me of where I am in life. God knew this is where I would be. Maybe not in this time or in this manner, but He knew my steps. He knew where I would be today and that I'm always in His plan.

Ask God for His will!

Inspirational Scripture

ENTRY BY: KIMBERLY BAILEY

DAY *56*

"[6]Be careful for nothing; but in everything by prayer and supplication with thanksgiving let your requests be made known unto God. [7]And the peace of God, which passeth all understanding, shall keep your hearts and minds in Christ Jesus."

—Philippians 4:6-7

Inspirational Quote

ENTRY BY: MIRANDA RIVERS

DAY *57*

"Healing starts from within."

"Pain changes your life forever; but so does healing from it."

—Author unknown

"Heal me, O Lord, and I shall be healed; Save me, and I shall be saved, For You *are* my praise."

—Jeremiah 17:14 (NKJV)

Inspirational Scripture

ENTRY BY: ESTHER BURGESS

DAY *58*

"The LORD God hath given me the tongue of the learned, that I should know how to speak a word in season to him that is weary: he wakeneth morning by morning, he wakeneth mine ear to hear as the learned."

—Isaiah 50:4

Inspirational Scripture

ENTRY BY: JESSIE STRIGGLES

DAY *59*

"Set me as a seal upon thine heart, as a seal upon thine arm: for love is strong as death; jealousy is cruel as the grave: the coals thereof are coals of fire, which hath a most vehement flame."

—Song of Solomon 8:6

JEALOUSY IS AS CRUEL AS THE GRAVE

Inspirational Scripture

ENTRY BY: ALICIA BAILEY

DAY *60*

"Do not be anxious about anything; but in every situation, by prayer and petition, with thanksgiving, present your requests to God. And the peace of God, which transcends all understanding, will guard your hearts and your minds in Christ Jesus."

—Philippians 4:6-7 (NIV)

These two verses in chapter four of Philippians empower us to begin to focus on our spiritual formation and not our problems. When we begin to keep our eyes on Jesus Christ, He will get the glory in our lives. When we commit to a lifestyle of prayer, there will be a shift in the atmosphere. In fact, the Apostle Paul mentioned that when we don't allow ourselves to be anxious, but begin to combine prayer with thanksgiving, we will experience a peace that transcends all understanding. WOW – that is the secret to decluttering our minds and releasing negative people and stuff of this world. It is time for us to walk in our own uniqueness and stand on the promises of God.

If you are taking the time to read this meditation, I want to encourage you. Why? Because it is my sincere desire that you strive to live an abundant life full of blessings and stop letting people or situations rob you of experiencing true peace. There are going to be times when life throws us unexpected curve balls, but we must stay focused and tell ourselves, "I will overcome". It is time for you to take control of your happiness and declare that no weapon formed against you shall prosper (Isaiah 54:17).

Prayer: Today, I am declaring that I am a child of the King, and I am not going to be anxious about anything, nor conform to the pressures of this world. Instead, I am going to spend time spiritually developing myself by staying close to my Lord and Savior.

Inspirational Quote

ENTRY BY: JAE (JOYCE) ROLLINS

DAY *61*

When the hand of the Lord is your keeper, He will cause your enemies to fight each other, while you praise into the greater. #praiseismyweapon

—Jae Rollins

Inspirational Affirmation

ENTRY BY: TREINNA THOMAS

DAY *62*

I AM ME!
OF WHOM I WILL ALWAYS LOVE
AND WILL ALWAYS CHERISH AND RESPECT.

—Treinna Thomas

Inspirational Affirmation

ENTRY BY: TENARIA DRUMMOND-SMITH

DAY *63*

You will never know what you're capable of doing until you try something. If you desire to write a book, maybe even start up a business, you have to first see yourself doing it in order for it to happen. Get yourself up and find out what others are doing. Write down a list of things that you're passionate about. This should help you decide what direction to go in. Kickstart a passion you've been sitting on for years. Work your faith because faith is all you need.

"[1]Now faith is the substance of things hoped for, the evidence of things not seen…[6]But without faith it is impossible to please him: for he that cometh to God must believe that he is, and that he is a rewarder of them that diligently seek him."

—Hebrews 11:1, 6

Inspirational Scripture

ENTRY BY: JACQUELENE SCRUGGS

DAY *64*

No matter what we are going through, we must always trust the Lord at His word because He tells us in Psalm 34:8: "O taste and see that the LORD is good: blessed is the man that trusteth in him."

Inspirational Affirmation

ENTRY BY: SOPHIA L. GREENE

DAY *65*

It is time to let go of hurt and pain. Now is the time to release energy that does not allow you to grow or travel with lightness. There is pain that travels so deep that it can be buried for years without acknowledging how it affects us going forward. Today, I choose to visit all my pain, I choose to feel all the hurt, and accept I am not exempt from pain. Today, I choose to forgive everyone that I thought, believed or knew would hurt me. I forgive, knowing that pain is a gift for the living.

Inspirational Scripture

ENTRY BY: THERESA BYRD

DAY *66*

"[1]Make a joyful noise unto the LORD, all ye lands. [2]Serve the LORD with gladness: come before his presence with singing. [3]Know ye that the LORD he is God: it is he that hath made us, and not we ourselves; we are his people, and the sheep of his pasture. [4]Enter into his gates with thanksgiving, and into his courts with praise: be thankful unto him, and bless his name. [5]For the LORD is good; his mercy is everlasting; and his truth endureth to all generations."

—Psalm 100:1-5

Inspirational Scripture

ENTRY BY: VERA MOORE

DAY *67*

[1]"I am the true vine, and my Father is the gardener. [2]He cuts off
every branch in me that bears no fruit, while every branch that
does bear fruit he prunes so that it will be even more fruitful. [3]You
are already clean because of the word I have spoken to you.
[4]Remain in me, as I also remain in you. No branch can bear fruit
by itself; it must remain in the vine. Neither can you bear fruit
unless you remain in me. [5]"I am the vine; you are the branches. If
you remain in me and I in you, you will bear much fruit; apart
from me you can do nothing.
[6]If you do not remain in me, you are like a branch that is thrown
away and withers; such branches are picked up, thrown into the
fire and burned. [7]If you remain in me and my words remain in
you, ask whatever you wish, and it will be done for you.

—John 15:1-7 (NIV)

I've learned to SURRENDER and REST in his word. We have no power, so give it up. You are not in control. God is the vine; we are the branches.

Inspirational Quote

Entry by: Leslie Duroseau

DAY *68*

You don't need to change the world.
You just need to change yourself.

—Leslie Duroseau

Inspirational Affirmation

ENTRY BY: LINDA M. JOHNSON

DAY *69*

GOD IS ALWAYS WITH YOU

A test is a challenge, dear sisters and brothers of the Most High God. God will not give us more than we can bear, and he will never leave us nor forsake us.

"My brethren, count it all joy when ye fall into divers temptations;"

—James 1:2

"Blessed is the man that endured temptation: for when he is tried, he shall receive the crown of life, which the Lord hath promised to them that love him."

—James 1:12

"Be strong and of a good courage, fear not, nor be afraid of them: for the LORD thy God, he it is that doth go with thee; he will not fail thee, nor forsake thee."

—Deuteronómy 31:6

Positive Thinking Will Make You Happy

Inspirational Affirmation

ENTRY BY: DAWN M. COLES

DAY *70*

TRUST IN THE LORD

"[5]Trust in the LORD with all your heart, And lean not on your own understanding; [6]In all your ways acknowledge Him, And He shall direct your paths."

—Proverbs 3:5-6 (NKJV)

The book of Proverbs was written by King Solomon, the son of David, who was asked by God in a dream what he would need to lead His people. Solomon requested wisdom. Of all the possible things he could've asked for, he asked for wisdom. So when the man whom God granted wisdom to wrote: "Trust in the Lord with all our hearts," it speaks volumes to me. I see it as God wanting us to gain understanding and knowledge while we continue to lean and trust in Him.

This scripture became so true to me when I was transitioning into a new job. I had so many mixed feelings about leaving a place of comfort and venturing out into the unknown. I'd interviewed successfully with three jobs. I asked the Lord for an answer and he said, "Trust me and chose the third offer." As the years progressed, the answer became clear. The two positions that I declined closed the unit of my specialty. So don't depend only upon your own judgment because it is limited. God sees into the future. Our Father is always eager to guide us on life's journey, but we must seek Him, acknowledge Him, and then listen for a response. God's heart is good towards us.

The most amazing thing about trusting in God and being obedient in your response is the blessing that flows. This divine place of employment introduced my daughter to a career in healthcare and built relationships with physicians who rendered optimum care to my mother and husband as he battled with cancer. It became a safe place for my family. A place where my grandchildren would be born. This employer became my extended family through life's journey. Relationships were established all by trusting in the LORD.

Inspirational Scripture

ENTRY BY: KENDRA RENEE' MANIGAULT

DAY 71

I'LL NEVER BE THE SAME AGAIN!

"Therefore if any man be in Christ, he is a new creature: old things are passed away; behold, all things become new."

—2 Corinthians 5:17

Inspirational Affirmation

ENTRY BY: LATRICIA T. DAVIS

DAY 72

RELATIONSHIPS

"Delight yourself also in the Lord, and He shall give you the desires of your heart."

—Psalm 37:4 (NKJV)

Relationships are what we make them to be. Most of the time, we have not defined or made clear the type of relationship that we desire to be in, or what we want in a relationship. I've found out that, sometimes, our expectations are set so high that they make it difficult to find anyone to measure up to our standards as a person. We expect a lot from the person we want to be in relationship with, but fail to give them what is expected of us. That's why we must learn to love and understand ourselves enough to know what we truly desire before we attempt to be in a relationship.

To avoid unnecessary hardship and heartache, it is in our best interests to truly define what we are willing to accept, and what we are willing to sacrifice. We must also find our self-worth; to know our true value and not allow anyone or anything make us feel as if we don't deserve the best. We must stop minimizing our value and capabilities in order to live up to someone's expectation of us. Then, and only then, will we be able to take our lives at the next level and achieve our goals as they relate to the types of relationships that we desire.

The Bible tells us to delight ourselves in Him. It is the Lord's will that we be in the right relationships, for He knows that it is not good for man to be alone, and He knows what's best for us. However, God wants us to be in relationship with Him, spending time, reading His Word and talking intimately with Him in prayer. That's what it means to delight in the Lord, and as we continue to do so, He gives us the desires of our hearts according to the will and plan that He has for our lives.

Inspirational Quote

ENTRY BY: CHERRYL SIMPSON

DAY 73

Worry is a thin stream of fear trickling through the mind. If encouraged, it cuts a channel into which all other thoughts are drained

—Arthur Somers Roche

We tend to cast our thought processes on what's not going too well. We say that we don't know how to meditate, but we do it every single time that we worry. Worry trickles into even our positive thoughts and causes a downward spiral into negativity. Thoughts become things! The watch that you have on your wrist was first a thought. It's the same as when we worry; sometimes we negatively meditate on something for so long that we see it come to fruition.

Guarding our hearts and minds works to protect them from these kinds of thoughts that will tend to do us harm in the end. For with our thoughts, we can become sick, and they can cause us to develop low self-esteem. Remember this: no one is born with confidence, it is developed. We have many resources at our fingertip these days and do not necessarily need a tangible Bible, because the Internet is viable and brings information to us in seconds with the click of a button. Learning to control our thoughts, by capturing them and replacing them with the Word of God, will help us to put your trust in God. God has given us the ability to create new things and to become the person whom He has created us to be. This takes surrender, obedience, and walking in faith. Sometimes you will not know where you are going, but in the end, if you trust Him, you will be on course. He will never let you down, for you are fearfully, and wonderfully made by Him and for His glory. Leave worry at the door and trust Him to show you true life, peace, joy, and grace in Him!

Inspirational Scripture

ENTRY BY: JEAN THOMPSON

DAY *74*

HAVE NO FEAR

"[1]The LORD is my light and my salvation; whom shall I fear? the LORD is the strength of my life; of whom shall I be afraid? [2]When the wicked, even mine enemies and my foes, came upon me to eat up my flesh, they stumbled and fell. [3]Though an host should encamp against me, my heart shall not fear: though war should rise against me, in this will I be confident."

"[7]Hear, O LORD, when I cry with my voice: have mercy also upon me, and answer me."

"[14]Wait on the LORD: be of good courage, and he shall strengthen thine heart: wait, I say, on the LORD."

—Psalm 27:1-3, 7, 14

Inspirational Scripture

Entry by: Antoinette Halsey

Day *75*

"Finally, brethren, whatsoever things are true, whatsoever things are honest, whatsoever things are just, whatsoever things are pure, whatsoever things are lovely, whatsoever things are of good report; if there be any virtue, and if there be any praise, think on these things."

—Philippians 4:8

Inspirational Scripture

Entry by: Tiffany D. Kelly

Day 76

"I can do all things through Christ who strengthens me."

—Philippians 4:13 (NKJV)

Inspirational Affirmation

ENTRY BY: NINA D. BROWN

DAY *77*

IF I TOLD YOU MY TRUTH (Joel 2:12-13)

If I told you my truth, what would you say? How would you look at me as I share my truth? Would you judge me and walk away? Or would you listen and embrace my truth as your own and help me navigate through it? Or would you laugh and talk about me?

This world has convinced me that I will never be what you say. Therefore, anger, bitterness, resentment, and brokenness have become my truth. I've lost my desire to be more than this moment. So, stop trying to make me change my truth. I'm disconnected, and this place is a reminder to keep my silent truth.

My truth is revenge, and the world needs to suffer as I have. I don't want to forgive, so stop asking me to. Others need to feel this pain and suffering. This is painful, and I want to be free, but this place has become my escape and safe place. My truth: I desire to be free from what has become my story, but how?

So today, I render my pain, sorrow, defeats, rejection, and failures. Help me find your truth. The truth that sets the captives free, the truth that changes my story to a testimony. The truth that plants me by the rivers of living waters. The truth of how your grace and mercy keep me, how your love saved me, and how your death restored me. How do I change my truth to tell others about a man who came to see about me and told me all about myself? He gave me a drink and now I have life, and I have life more abundantly.

Lord, today I seek your face, asking you to help me find the real truth.

Inspirational Quote

ENTRY BY: KEEVA DEDEWO

DAY *78*

In every dream journey, there comes a moment when you have to quit living as if the purpose of life is to arrive safely at death.

—Mark Batterson

Inspirational Quote

ENTRY BY: DAWN GRANTHAM

DAY *79*

Optimism is the faith that leads to achievement.

—Helen Keller

Dreams still come true, so believe and have faith. Don't be intimidated because of what they are saying. Everyone is not for you. Remember, they still criticize God, and look what he has created.

Inspirational Affirmation

Entry by: Roberta Jones-Johnson

Day *80*

God won't give you
—more—
than you can bear.

Inspirational Affirmation

ENTRY BY: BERNETTA GREEN

DAY *81*

HEALED

Lord, thank you for your healing mercy. You continue to restore my soul. I shall continue to walk upright in your virtue. Purge my soul from all things not of You. Today, I am healed…today, I am victorious…

HALLELUJAH, HALLELUJAH, HALLELUJAH!!!

Inspirational Scripture

Entry by: Debra D. Carter

Day *82*

"Many women do noble things, but you surpass them all." Charm is deceptive, and beauty is fleeting; but a woman who fears the Lord is to be praised."

—Proverbs 31:29-30 (NIV)

I dedicate this to my beloved mom, who planted the seeds of faith, prayer, unconditional love, and of knowing that God is real. I carry her strong spirit and wisdom with me every day.

Inspirational Scripture

ENTRY BY: KAREN M. CARTER

DAY *83*

"This is what the LORD says: 'Stand at the crossroads and look; ask for the ancient paths, ask where the good way is, and walk in it, and you will find rest for your souls'..."

—Jeremiah 6-16[a] (NIV)

Inspirational Scripture

ENTRY BY: SHERELL FERRER

DAY *84*

"I will praise thee; for I am fearfully and wonderfully made: marvellous are thy works; and that my soul knoweth right well."

—Psalm 139:14

SELF-ESTEEM

As a teen, I suffered from low self-esteem. My lips were too big, my hair was too short, my body was too skinny, and the list went on. It wasn't until I came into the realization that we were all uniquely made by God, and he makes no mistakes, that I now embrace all of my flaws because they make me the woman I am today.

Inspirational Affirmation

ENTRY BY: ROSEMARY HART

DAY *85*

Destiny drives desire.

It is not how fast one achieves; it is finishing what you've started. Never give up!

—Rosemary Hart

Inspirational Scripture

ENTRY BY: DEBORAH PERRY

DAY *86*

"Train up a child in the way he should go: and when his is old, he will not depart from it."

—Proverbs 22:6

This Scripture speaks about training up a child in the way they should go. I based raising and training my children according to the Bible, just the way my parents did. My mother raised me and my siblings according to the Bible, teaching us the Word, believing God, and putting Him first. I always felt and still believe that this helps with the success of my life, as well as for my children. Putting the fear of God, the trust of God, and faith in God before them, and allowing them to build on that, guaranteed their future of success.

The way of the Lord is the greatest recipe for raising children.

Inspirational Quote

ENTRY BY: KIMBERLY BAILEY

DAY *87*

God never said the journey would be easy, but He did say that the arrival would be worthwhile.

—Max Lucado

Inspirational Quote

ENTRY BY: MIRANDA RIVERS

DAY *88*

The Love Bits

One of the most beautiful qualities of true friendship is to understand and be understood.

—Lucius Annaeus Seneca

"Love is patient, love is kind. It does not envy, it does not boast, it is not proud. It does not dishonor others, it is not self-seeking, it is not easily angered, it keeps no record of wrongs."

—1 Corinthians 13:4-6 (NIV)

Inspirational Quote

ENTRY BY: ESTHER BURGESS

DAY *89*

I learned that what happened to me did not have to define who I was. My past could not control my future unless I allowed it to.

—Joyce Meyer

Inspirational Affirmation

ENTRY BY: JESSIE STRIGGLES

DAY *90*

SICKNESSES CAME TO TAKE ME OUT, BUT MERCY SAID "NO!"

—Jessie Striggles

Inspirational Scripture

ENTRY BY: ALICIA BAILEY

DAY *91*

"I am smart! I will pass the test! I am beautiful! I am confident! I can do all things through Christ who strengthens me!"

Every morning before my precious teenage daughter Adrianna departs from home, we engage in dialogue by reciting the above affirmation. These words were selected by me to build her confidence and her character. I am a firm believer that we are called to lift each other up. Our young people need to be encouraged, and we need to affirm that they are smart and beautiful. The Word of God states: "Train up a child in the way he should go, and when he is old, he will not depart from it." (Prov 22:6)

My daughter needs to know she is "fearfully and wonderfully made" (Psalm 139:14). She needs to be empowered to dream, to have visions, and to have aspirations. She needs to be equipped spiritually, mentally, and physically to conquer any obstacle she may encounter in this life's journey.

We must ensure we are showering our youth with positive affirmations to help them be strong, to have the ability to make sound decisions, and to have healthy minds, bodies, and souls. We want them to walk by faith and not by sight (2 Co 5:7). We want them to reach for the stars and climb every mountain of opportunity, if it's God's will. We want them to never give up or lose hope. We want them to know that God is the Author and Finisher of their Faith. We want them to know when they need to walk away from people who want to keep them from growing up to be a king or queen. We want them to know they can do all things through Christ who strengthens them (Philippians 4:13).

Our children belong to us. It is our duty to ensure that we are raising a generation that will be powerful, yet humble and grateful. Remember, we must love them no matter what happens in life. We are called to teach, to nurture, and lead our young people by example. The next time you see a young person, speak life-changing words.

Inspirational Quote

Entry by: Jae (Joyce) Rollins

Day *92*

That day when the Lord whispers in your ear, open your eyes and see what has already been done! #provider

—Jae Rollins

Inspirational Quote

ENTRY BY: TREINNA THOMAS

DAY *93*

The more you resist, the more your issues and/or problems will persist. Pray when you must face a challenge and allow God to handle your battle; otherwise, the challenge will remain.

—Treinna Thomas

Inspirational Affirmation

ENTRY BY: TENARIA DRUMMOND-SMITH

DAY *94*

Many people have been diagnosed with illnesses such as high blood pressure, cancer, sickle cell anemia, addictions, depression, and the list goes on. Some people are born with illnesses, while some illnesses are brought on by how we treat our bodies and how we eat. But know that illness doesn't have to be a death sentence. It starts by making better choices for ourselves and getting help.

"But he was wounded for our transgressions, he was bruised for our iniquities: the chastisement of our peace was upon him; and with his stripes we are healed."

—Isaiah 53:5

God is still in the business of healing. Do you believe He can still do it for you? God took the beating for you and me, so we don't have to suffer. God's word is truth.

"[20]And, behold, a woman, which was diseased with an issue of blood twelve years, came behind him, and touched the hem of his garment: [21]For she said within herself, If I may but touch his garment, I shall be whole. [22]But Jesus turned him about, and when he saw her, he said, Daughter, be of good comfort; thy faith hath made thee whole. And the woman was made whole from that hour."

—Matthew 9:20-22

Inspirational Scripture

ENTRY BY: JACQUELENE SCRUGGS

DAY *95*

Man will let you down but God will never turn his back on you, and I know this to be true.

"The LORD is my light and my salvation; whom shall I fear? The LORD is the strength of my life; of whom shall I be afraid?"

—Psalm 27:1

Inspirational Affirmation

ENTRY BY: SOPHIA L. GREENE

DAY *96*

Why is she not participating? Why is she not accepting our invitation? She used to be one of our treasured supporters. This does not make any sense! Who is going to entertain us while allowing us to sit back and watch a great drama that's designed to destroy all the participants? The audacity to send us this note!

"Dear Anger, I must decline your invitation for breakfast, lunch, or dinner. We have been friends for a long time, however, I have no appetite for the meals that are being served."

Inspirational Scripture

ENTRY BY: THERESA BYRD

DAY *97*

[1]Hear my cry, O God; attend unto my prayer. [2]From the end of
the earth will I cry unto thee, when my heart is overwhelmed: lead
me to the rock that is higher than I.
[3]For thou hast been a shelter for me, and a strong tower from the
enemy. [4]I will abide in thy tabernacle for ever: I will trust in the
covert of thy wings. Selah. [5]For thou, O God, hast heard my
vows: thou hast given me the heritage of those that fear thy
name. [6]Thou wilt prolong the king's life: and his years as many
generations. [7]He shall abide before God for ever: O prepare
mercy and truth, which may preserve him. [8]So will I sing praise
unto thy name for ever, that I may daily perform my vows.

—Psalm 61:1-8

Inspirational Scripture

ENTRY BY: VERA MOORE

DAY *98*

"[5]Trust in the LORD with all thine heart; and lean not unto thine own understanding. [6]In all they ways acknowledge him, and he shall direct thy paths. [7]Be not wise in thine own eyes: fear the LORD, and depart from evil."

—Proverbs 3:5-7

My faith and trust in God have sustained me in all my herculean challenges. Being the first, a trailblazer in many arenas, is not easy. You need the power of the Holy Ghost behind you.

It's funny. In the natural, we ask people for advice, we seek consultations, and we go to seminars (it's all good). However, why don't we ask HIM? He says "...seek ye first the kingdom of God, and his righteousness; and all these things shall be added unto you." (Matthew 6:33) He won't gossip or tell your enemies. Remember the song "What A Friend We Have In Jesus"? ASK HIM. He's YOUR FRIEND.

Inspirational Scripture

Entry by: Leslie Duroseau

DAY *99*

"[23]Search me, O God, and know my heart; test me and know my anxious thoughts. [24]Point out anything in me that offends you, and lead me along the path of everlasting life."

—Psalm 139:23-24 (NLT)

Inspirational Affirmation

ENTRY BY: LINDA M. JOHNSON

DAY *100*

WALK IN THE SPIRIT

Lord, renew my mind daily. Lord, renew my heart daily. Lord, sanctify my soul daily. Dear God, impart into me the goodness that comes from the fruits of your spirit. My body is the temple of the Holy Spirit. This is my daily prayer.

"Let this mind be in you, which was also in Christ Jesus:"

—Philippians 2:5

"But the fruit of the spirit is love, joy, peace, longsuffering, gentleness, goodness, faith, meekness, temperance: against such there is no law. And they that are Christ's have crucified the flesh with the affections and lusts. If we live in the Spirit, let us also walk in the Spirit."

—Galatians 5:22-25 (KJV)

I desire to be God's woman. A virtuous woman is hard to find (Proverbs 31).

Positive Thinking Will Make You Happy

Inspirational Scripture

ENTRY BY: DAWN M. COLES

DAY *101*

OBEDIENCE

"[4]When He had stopped speaking, He said to Simon, 'Launch out into the deep and let down your nets for a catch.' [5]But Simon answered and said to Him, 'Master, we have toiled all night and caught nothing; nevertheless at Your word I will let down the net.' [6]And when they had done this, they caught a great number of fish, and their net was breaking. [7]So they signaled to their partners in the other boat to come and help them. And they came and filled both the boats, so that they began to sink."

—Luke 5:4-7 (NKJV)

Obedience in some form or shape can be a bit difficult for some. It's a daily struggle of deciding to submit your will unto the Lord. One step of obedience to His word will bring you closer to Him so you can be amazed in His presence. Obedience is proof of your faith and trust in God alone. You cannot move forward in a standstill or parked position. An open heart to God is required to move forward in obedience. It may not make sense or feel good, but His rewards are priceless.

Inspirational Scripture

ENTRY BY: KENDRA RENEE' MANIGAULT

DAY *102*

GREATNESS LIES BENEATH

"Little children, you are from God and have overcome them, for he who is in you is greater than he who is in the world."

—1John 4:4 (ESV)

Inspirational Scripture

ENTRY BY: LATRICIA T. DAVIS

DAY 103

MY HELP

"[1]I will lift up mine eyes unto the hills, from whence cometh my help.
[2]My help cometh from the LORD, which made heaven and earth.
[3]He will not suffer thy foot to be moved: he that keepeth thee will not
slumber. [4]Behold, he that keepeth Israel shall neither slumber nor
sleep. [5]The LORD is thy keeper: the LORD is thy shade upon thy right
hand. [6]The sun shall not smite thee by day, nor the moon by night.
[7]The LORD shall preserve thee from all evil: he shall preserve thy
soul. [8]The LORD shall preserve thy going out and thy coming in from
this time forth, and even for evermore."

—Psalm 121

If it had not been for the LORD on my side, I don't know where I would be. No matter what you may be going through today as you read this passage of scripture, trust and know that all the help you need comes from the Lord. No problem, situation, or circumstance is too hard for God. Nothing is impossible for Him; there is no failure in Him. God will give you the strength that you need to stand in the midst of the storm. He will preserve your soul and keep you from falling as you acknowledge Him in all things. He's a twenty-four-hour God who never slumbers or sleeps.

Don't be afraid to call on His name. Ask anything in His name and He will certainly answer you. There's an old Christian saying: "He's an on-time God. He may not come when you want Him, but He's always on time." He's never failed me yet. When you feel overwhelmed, and when you are not sure what about what to do in any situation, lift your eyes up to the hills and remember where your HELP comes from.

Inspirational Quote

ENTRY BY: CHERRYL SIMPSON

DAY *104*

"The graveyard is the richest place on earth, because it is here that you will find all the hopes and dreams that were never fulfilled, the books that were never written, the songs that were never sung, the inventions that were never shared, the cures that were never discovered, all because someone was too afraid to take that first step, keep with the problem, or determined to carry out their dream."

—Les Brown

We are created specifically for a purpose. Even though we should develop our talents, skills, and abilities, we are not here to help ourselves. We have a fingerprint that no one else in the entire world will have, and that means we are each special in His eyes. He made no mistakes in creating each of us. Even identical twins have differences. In understanding that we are here for a purpose, what should we do about it? Most of us are in jobs that someone else wanted us to be in, or just because it pays the bills. What if you decided to invest in yourself and find out what you do well? What if you went to work and you felt like you were not at work because it was too much fun? What if you spent a day with someone and shared that gift with them, and it caused them to excel? We all have talents, skill, and abilities that will change this world!

Some of you are afraid of your uniqueness, for fear that someone will laugh or mock you, but do not be afraid. Push yourself forward into the destiny that was created for you, a life that's fulfilling, successful, and purposeful. If you don't share it with the world, you will feel a void inside of you. You will bring to this world what no one else has ever thought about before. No one can copy your special way of doing it! You were created just for this purpose so be inspired, be transparent, and be fearless! You have this thing called life in the right perspective, and it needs you! "Higher" is calling you!

Inspirational Scripture

ENTRY BY: JEAN THOMPSON

DAY *105*

FAITH

"1Therefore being justified by faith, we have peace with God
through our Lord Jesus Christ: 2By whom also we have access by
faith into this grace wherein we stand, and rejoice in hope of the
glory of God. 3And not only so, but we glory in tribulations also:
knowing that tribulation worketh patience;
4And patience, experience; and experience, hope: 5And hope
maketh not ashamed; because the love of God is shed abroad in
our hearts by the Holy Ghost which is given unto us. 6For when we
were yet without strength, in due time Christ died for the ungodly.
7For scarcely for a righteous man will one die: yet peradventure for
a good man some would even dare to die. 8But God commendeth
his love toward us, in that, while we were yet sinners, Christ died
for us."

—Romans 5:1-8

Inspirational Scripture

ENTRY BY: ANTOINETTE HALSEY

DAY *106*

"The LORD is my light and my salvation; whom shall I fear? the LORD is the strength of my life; of whom shall I be afraid?"

—Psalm 27:1

Inspirational Quote

ENTRY BY: TIFFANY D. KELLY

DAY *107*

Be patient with the process. Change doesn't always happen overnight. Stop blaming the enemy when it's just God seeing how much you trust His process. It's only a test. Hang in there. Your breakthrough is coming!

—Tiffany D. Kelly

ENTRY BY: NINA D. BROWN

DAY *108*

THE POWER WITHIN

"Power is Determination Speaking What Silence Created."

There is no blueprint, manual, or Lifetime movie to help you navigate this life. We all would like a two-hour special where the problem is fixed, the day is saved, and everyone is in love, crying, and kissing. Baby, wake up, wash your face and look in the mirror. This life right here, the one you are living, you will need to figure this out and no two-hour movie is going to provide you the answer. It is hard, painful, unbearable, and giving up at times will be the right and only answer, but there is a power within.

See, the power you need does not come from friends or how-to-books. It comes from the notes you have from traceable references. Okay, don't believe me? Go to the mirror and look into your own eyes. Take your reference notes out for a quick review. Think and reflect for a moment. See the reference notes for dates and times of troubles, painful events, and unexpected life changes. Remember how the pain was unbearable, the cuts were deep, the medication did not help, and how your pain addicted you to the thing that was trying to break you. The situation left you with some black and blue marks, stitches, and maybe a scar or two.

Now, there is no trace of war or proof of a fight. Nothing other than reference points of your survival. The reality is that you are still standing because He has placed a power inside of you. The power within has proven time and time again that quitting was not your option. No matter the scars upon your life, you are a limited addition.

Inspirational Quote

Entry by: Keeva Dedewo

Day *109*

When in lack, imagine your prosperity.

—Keeva Dedewo

Inspirational Scripture

ENTRY BY: DAWN GRANTHAM

DAY *110*

"Now faith is the substance of things hoped for, the evidence of things not seen."

—Hebrews 11:1

Inspirational Quote

ENTRY BY: ROBERTA JONES-JOHNSON

DAY *111*

My husband is my king, I am his queen, and God is King over all.

—Roberta Jones-Johnson

Inspirational Affirmation

ENTRY BY: BERNETTA GREEN

DAY *112*

DELIVERANCE

O merciful Creator of all things great and small, hallowed be thy name. Father, you continue to keep me in your warm embrace, you continue to shower me with your blessings, and you continue to guide me. Father, place your countenance upon me, deliver me from all evil, and humble me so I can do thy will. Lord, I pray that you deliver me from all strongholds not of you. Amen.

—Bernetta Green

Inspirational Quote

ENTRY BY: DEBRA D. CARTER

DAY *113*

"Dad, your guiding hand on my shoulder will remain with me forever."

—Author unknown

Fathers lay the foundation for the kind of men their young daughters will perceive to be potential mates.

—Debra Carter

Thank you, Daddy, for leading by example with your thoughts, words, and deeds.

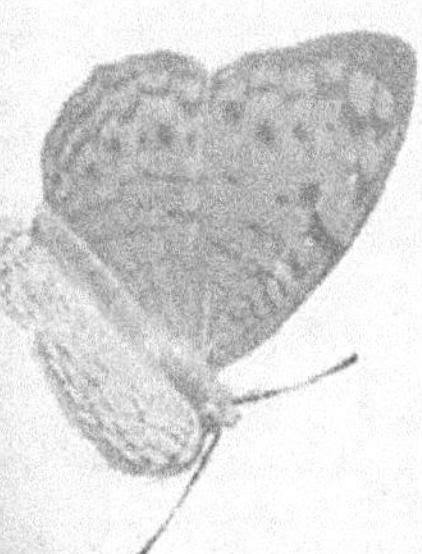

D̲edication
A̲sset in my life
D̲evotion
D̲ivine inspiration
Y̲our love

Inspirational Scripture

ENTRY BY: KAREN M. CARTER

DAY *114*

"Whether you turn to the right or to the left, your ears will hear a voice behind you, saying, 'This is the way; walk in it.'"

—Isaiah 30:21 (NIV)

Inspirational Affirmation

ENTRY BY: SHERELL FERRER

DAY *115*

Love yourself enough to take the actions required for your happiness...

Love yourself enough to cut yourself loose from the ties of the drama-filled past...

Love yourself enough to move on!

—Dr. Steve Maraboli

Inspirational Affirmation

ENTRY BY: ROSEMARY HART

DAY *116*

PREPARE

Invest time, effort and unwavering commitment to realizing your dreams.

—Rosemary Hart

Inspirational Affirmation

ENTRY BY: DEBORAH PERRY

DAY *117*

"Let this mind be in you, which was also in Christ Jesus:"

—Philippians 2:5

I live my life by this scripture. I believe that the God in me directs me, covers me, and keeps me. When I trust Him, believe in Him and do according to what the Bible says, then all my steps are ordered by Him. My mother always said to me; "Follow your first mind, and if your mind is in Jesus, never think anything is a mistake."

Think of it as all things happening for a reason. Sometimes things may not go our way, but we must know it's the way of God. Even when we think something is wrong, my mother used to say that when you follow your first mind, you can't blame anyone but yourself. But if you follow your first mind and it's like God's, you have no one to blame. Your response will be, "Lord, thank you for allowing me to go through this and make it through." There is something better in store for me.

Clear your mind.

Inspirational Quote

ENTRY BY: KIMBERLY BAILEY

DAY *118*

A mother is a woman who shows you the light, when you just see the dark.

—Grimaldos Robin

Inspirational Quote

ENTRY BY: MIRANDA RIVERS

DAY *119*

I am the best me I can be daily.

Your mind is a powerful thing when you fill it with positive thoughts, your life will start to change.

—Unknown

"As iron sharpens iron, so one person sharpens another."

—Proverbs 27:17 (NIV)

Inspirational Quote

ENTRY BY: ESTHER BURGESS

DAY *120*

Grace is the power of the Holy Spirit coming to us free of charge to enable you to do with ease what you could never do on your own with any amount of struggle and effort.

—Joyce Meyer

Inspirational Affirmation

ENTRY BY: JESSIE STRIGGLES

DAY *121*

Sit still and see the salvation of the Lord, I am cushioning the blows, the way of escape has already been made.

"NO WEAPON FORMED THAT IS FORMED AGAINST THEE SHALL PROSPER;"

—Isaiah 54:17

Inspirational Affirmation

ENTRY BY: ALICIA BAILEY

DAY *122*

YOU ARE SO SPECIAL

Do you realize how special you are? Well, let me take the time to tell you why I believe you are. You were created in God's image. You are unique. You are a rare gem, and you are one of a kind! The Word of God states in Jeremiah 1:5 (NKJV) "Before I formed you in the womb I knew you, before you were born I set you apart; I appointed you as a prophet to the nations." You were born to survive and to be different. You should not embark on a mission to be a copycat; be an original.

I believe that we have been called to live our life to the fullest. I am not suggesting that we will not encounter any challenges and our lives will be without struggles, but I am saying that you are somebody, so get up and live. Take time to smile, laugh hard, go on vacations, have fun, pamper yourself, free your mind, hang out with yourself, have a positive attitude, and be happy.

Because you are so special, I want you to pause and think about that assignment or project you were charged to complete, but you have not completed it. What vision have you shut down because you have been blinded by people and things of this world? What dreams have you deferred because you have been waiting for the perfect time? What resolutions have you set every New Year's Day, but have yet to become reality? What SMART goals have you declared, but are still only written down on paper? Well, the time has come, don't delay any longer, pause and reflect and begin to fulfill your purpose. You need to go for it! You are so special, and I need you to really put that in your spirit. You are worthy, and you define who you are. Even if you had some setbacks or failures, it is alright. It is time to spread your wings and soar like an eagle.

Inspirational Quote

ENTRY BY: JAE (JOYCE) ROLLINS

DAY *123*

In ministry, the weight of a title will sometimes cause pain, but God will show up and cause things to call into order #theorderofGod

—Jae Rollins

Inspirational Quote

ENTRY BY: TREINNA THOMAS

DAY *124*

Mindfulness
—relax your mind and embrace peace from within. It is at that moment you can be one with self and find the true essence of who you are.

—Treinna Thomas

Inspirational Affirmation

ENTRY BY: TENARIA DRUMMOND-SMITH

DAY *125*

Sometimes you have to take a good look in the mirror and encourage yourself when there's no one around to tell you how everything's going to be alright. People will talk about you and lie on you for no good reason. That's the nature of people, and oftentimes, it comes from people who are closest to you. It can be your spouse, your children, your siblings, even the people you fellowship with. These are things everyone deals with in their everyday lives.

"For we wrestle not against flesh and blood, but against principalities, against powers, against the rulers of the darkness of this world, against spiritual wickedness in high places."

—Ephesians 6:12

YOU could also have offended someone, so I encourage you to go to that person and make things right. If God can forgive us for our sins, we can also forgive one another. And if the person you offended doesn't want to accept your apology, keep it moving.

"For if ye forgive men their trespasses, your heavenly Father will also forgive you: But if ye forgive not men their trespasses, neither will your Father forgive your trespasses."

—Matthew 6:14-15

Inspirational Scripture

ENTRY BY: JACQUELENE SCRUGGS

DAY *126*

No matter what we have, no matter what we accomplish, we ought to give God all the praise and the glory.

"[5]Trust in the Lord with all thine heart; and lean not unto thine own understanding. [6]In all thy ways acknowledge him, and he shall direct thy paths."

—Proverbs 3:5-6

Inspirational Affirmation

ENTRY BY: SOPHIA L. GREENE

DAY *127*

Who told you, you are not worthy of love and respect? Who told you that your steps do not carry the energy of love that encompasses change? Who told you that you carry nothing within? Who told you that size and color determine that you win? Hey sister! Yes, you! Excuse me, yo my brother! Throw that mirror of orchestrated lies away, take a look at beauty, strength, and depth of anything you need to win. Yes, it's you, it's me, and we are here and designed to win.

Inspirational Scripture

ENTRY BY: THERESA BYRD

DAY *128*

"No weapon that is formed against thee shall prosper; and every tongue that shall rise against thee in judgment thou shalt condemn. This is the heritage of the servants of the LORD, and their righteousness is of me, saith the LORD."

—Isaiah 54:17

Inspirational Scripture

ENTRY BY: VERA MOORE

DAY *129*

"[17]O God, thou hast taught me from my youth: and hitherto have I declared thy wondrous works. [18]Now also when I am old and greyheaded, O God, forsake me not; until I have shewed thy strength unto this generation, and thy power to every one that is to come."

— Psalm 71:17-18

I was raised with a loving mother and father who had a relationship with Christ and taught me early. This solid foundation from the beginning is, was, and will always be my strength.

Teach one, reach one, touch one.

Let JESUS be the CEO of your business. We are a work in progress. God is the finisher.

Inspirational Affirmation

ENTRY BY: LESLIE DUROSEAU

DAY *130*

This is one of the hardest lessons to learn. Often, we are too busy trying to change and fix everyone else that we fail to work on ourselves. I love doing for others. It's in my DNA. Serving others, helping others, and making opportunities available for others is what I do professionally and in my personal life. I can remember being this way from a very young girl. I always gave my last, and too much of myself to others. I always wanted to make others feel good. By being there for others, you guessed it: I would forget about myself. Being there for others can be gratifying, but it is also demanding and tiresome.

I think a time comes in most of our lives that we have that "AHA!" moment or we have another type of moment. One in which we crash and burn, get frustrated, angry, or just want to give up. Hopefully for you, this is your "AHA!" moment. The one in which you realize that you are just as important, worthy, and deserving as everyone else. You took a pause and began to focus on yourself.

I found the best way to do that for myself was to take my rest in the Lord. While resting in the Lord, I had to learn how to become totally dependent upon Him. I reevaluated myself and how I was doing things, how I was living, and even more so, how I was merely existing. For all the good I believed I was doing by helping and serving others, I forgot about myself, and I did not realize it. I believed I was doing what I was supposed to do, and more importantly, what I believed God wanted me to do.

Finally, it dawned on me. For all the ways I wanted to please God, for all the good I believed I should do for others, and for all the great changes I wanted to see happen in the world, I realized that it would never truly happen for me if it did not begin within me. The change I want for others, and for the world, must begin within me first. I change the world by making myself the priority in my life. I change the world by working with God, and not as a lone ranger, and I change the world by becoming authentically "me."

Inspirational Affirmation

Entry by: Linda M. Johnson

Day *131*

GOD'S DIVINE PROTECTION OVER MY CHILDREN

The love beyond my wound is my cry out to the Lord to save, sanctify, deliver, and protect my children from sin. For God has a purpose and a perfect plan for their lives. Father, I thank you for your divine protection, and I think you for encamping my children around and about with your ministering angels (Psalm 91).

Positive Thinking Will Make You Happy

Inspirational Scripture

ENTRY BY: DAWN M. COLES

DAY *132*

PRAYER OF VICTORY

"[1]May the LORD answer you (David) in the day of trouble! May the name of the God of Jacob set you securely on high [and defend you in battle]! [2]May He send you help from the sanctuary (His dwelling place) And support and strengthen you from Zion! [3]May He remember all your meal offerings and accept your burnt offering. Selah. [4]May He grant you your heart's desire and fulfill all your plans. [5]We will sing joyously over your victory, and in the name of our God we will set up our banners. May the LORD fulfill all your petitions. [6]Now I know that the LORD saves His anointed; He will answer him from His holy heaven with the saving strength of His right hand. [7]Some trust in chariots and some in horses, but we will remember and trust in the name of the LORD our God."

—Psalm 20:1-7 (AMP)

After a day of many challenges and oppositions, I praise the God that I put my trust in. He is faithful over his word and sends his ministering angels to strengthen us when we call upon him in our time of need. Let us sing joyous songs of victory. The name of God is our banner. The Lord has heard our petitions. We can shout out in strength and will be victorious.

Inspirational Scripture

ENTRY BY: KENDRA RENEE' MANIGAULT

DAY *133*

GOD'S THOUGHTS TOWARD US MATTERS!

"I know what I'm doing. I have it all planned out-plans to take care of you, not abandon you, plans to give you the future you hope for."

—Jeremiah 29:11 (MSG)

Inspirational Scripture

ENTRY BY: LATRICIA T. DAVIS

DAY *134*

I CAN DO ALL THINGS

"I can do all things through Christ which strengtheneth me."

—Philippians 4:13

There is nothing in this world that we cannot accomplish. It may be difficult at times to understand and be content in the state or place that we find ourselves in. However, be encouraged to know that you are not alone, so don't give up. Don't throw in the towel because through Jesus Christ, you can do all things! He will give you the strength to move forward and accomplish all that you aspire to do in life. I believe that God has gifted every one of his creation with assignments and specific talents that are unique to each individual. Sometimes we known what they are but find it difficult getting the process started, but be encouraged. God knows where you are in the process. With Him, all things are possible. May you find contentment and consolation in this scripture to ease the self-imposed stress that we often place on ourselves because we simply fail to believe.

Philippians 4:13 is one of many favorite scriptures that I use to encourage and speak over my life daily because it reminds me that I need the strength of the God to help me accomplish all my dreams, goals, and aspirations. It gets hard at times as situations and circumstances keep occurring. Life can leave you feeling as if the sun will never shine again. Be encouraged today, knowing that the pain and suffering that we experience will eventually come to an end. Use God's Word and declare it, decree it, speak it over your life every day: "I CAN DO ALL THINGS THROUGH CHRIST THAT STRENGTHENS ME". BELIEVE THAT YOU CAN IN JESUS CHRIST.

Inspirational Quote

ENTRY BY: CHERRYL SIMPSON

DAY *135*

If you're still looking for that one person who can change your life, take a look in the mirror.

—Romy Ras

Change is necessary for our growth, and the only person who can change you is yourself! Most of us usually have to go through a crisis before we submit to change, but this is not necessary. The fact that we are granted another day is an indication that we are given another chance. Someone did not wake up today. All it takes is getting up every day and doing something different, because if we keep doing the same thing, we will have the same results. Reading and learning is essential for our growth.

Prior to my divorce, I heard that nothing will change until you do. It initially didn't make sense to me until I realized that if I don't change, every single thing will remain the same. I expected someone else to change but that never happened. It doesn't even matter if they are doing right or wrong; until you change, things will always remain the same. You are the creator within your life because you were given the authority to create by God. He has given you every single thing that you need and it's inside of you!

But first, you've first got to get up and listen, and this is the hard part. There is so much distraction around you, but getting in a quiet place, meditating on His word, and listening will get you where you need to be on a daily basis. Somethings you will not understand, but when you look back, you will know what He was doing. So trust Him and trust the process as you go through the choice to change. You are your greatest asset, and your gift is right inside of you. Delano Johnson stated in his book, *Refuse to Live Talented and Broke*, "Living the life of your dreams starts with waking up." (21).

Inspirational Scripture

ENTRY BY: JEAN THOMPSON

DAY *136*

PROSPERITY

"[1]Blessed is the man that walketh not in the counsel of the ungodly, nor standeth in the way of sinners, nor sitteth in the seat of the scornful. [2]But his delight is in the law of the Lord; and in his law doth he meditate day and night. [3]And he shall be like a tree planted by the rivers of water, that bringeth forth his fruit in his season; his leaf also shall not wither; and whatsoever he doeth shall prosper."

—Psalm 1:1-3

Inspirational Scripture

ENTRY BY: ANTOINETTE HALSEY

DAY *137*

"One thing have I desired of the LORD, that will I seek after; that I may dwell in the house of the LORD all the days of my life, to behold the beauty of the LORD, and to enquire in his temple."

—Psalm 27:4

Inspirational Scripture

ENTRY BY: TIFFANY D. KELLY

DAY *138*

"So do not fear, for I am with you; do not be dismayed, for I am your God. I will strengthen you and help you; I will uphold you with my righteous right hand."

—Isaiah 41:10 (NIV)

Inspirational Affirmation

ENTRY BY: NINA D. BROWN

DAY *139*

SHE NEVER SPOKE A WORD

"Sometimes the Greatest Revelation comes from the Simplicity of a Few Words"

The busyness of the café set the momentum for the loud conversations and outburst of uncontrolled laughter. Then SHE entered the café, and for a split second, the room went silent. Everything knew to embrace this moment. There has to be a realignment of time as it was presented into a new space.

SHE took Her seat, and the entire space embodied Her very essence, submitting itself to Her every thought. This space understood the importance of the power connected to Her very presence. SHE never parted Her lips, yet the room obeyed and meet the demands of Her every need as the space provided Her with all SHE wanted. Time honored and understood Her presence as it respected Her position in this space as it rested within the scope of each passing second.

Time knew Her presence at this very moment would present the simplicity of a few words, creating the greatest impact on the very place she now occupied. Time provided to all those around this moment the greatest revelation to them that sought to understand Her very essence.

Your words are just a reaffirmation of the verbal identification connected to the physical presentation before your personal introduction to the very space you now stand. Your silence affirms your strength as it demonstrates your power. Your silence tells your story to those who have been granted an ear to listen as they hear your truth. Your silence provides an actual record of the dates and times of your survival and provides you the proof of your testimony. Her/YOUR silence never speaks a word. It commands others to speak.

Inspirational Scripture

ENTRY BY: KEEVA DEDEWO

DAY *140*

"Pray without ceasing."

—1 Thessalonians 5:17

Inspirational Quote

ENTRY BY: DAWN GRANTHAM

DAY *141*

March to the beat of Jesus.

—Dawn Grantham

It simply means don't try to live life like anyone else, but to live life the way God the creator would want you to live. Living his way is trusting him to lead and guide you, throughout the day, no matter what obstacles occur.

Inspirational Affirmation

ENTRY BY: ROBERTA JONES-JOHNSON

DAY *142*

God gave us two ears and one mouth, so listen twice as much as you speak!

—Roberta Jones-Johnson

Inspirational Scripture

ENTRY BY: BERNETTA GREEN

DAY *143*

"[1]If thou wilt return, O Israel, saith the LORD, return unto me: and if thou wilt put away thine abominations out of my sight, then shalt thou not remove. [2]And thou shalt swear, The LORD liveth, in truth, in judgment, and in righteousness; and the nations shall bless themselves in him, and in him shall they glory."

—Jeremiah 4:1-2

Inspirational Quote

ENTRY BY: DEBRA D. CARTER

DAY *144*

God, grant me the serenity
to accept the things
I cannot change,

Courage to change the
things I can, and the
wisdom to know the difference.

—Reinhold Niebuhr

Inspirational Quote

ENTRY BY: KAREN M. CARTER

DAY *145*

Climb Ev'ry Mountain

Climb ev'ry mountain
Search high and low
Follow ev'ry by-way
Every path you know

Climb ev'ry mountain
Ford ev'ry stream
Follow ev'ry rainbow
'Till you find your dream

—Songwriters Oscar II Hammerstein & Richard Rodgers

Inspirational Affirmation

ENTRY BY: SHERELL FERRER

DAY *146*

LIFE AFTER A LOSS

I have experienced many joyful days in my life, and August 26th, 2008 was one of the most joyous days of my life. God finally answered my prayers and blessed me with a baby boy. This was a miracle after having five girls. God granted me my deepest heart's desire, but at only five months, he was diagnosed with a rare sickness called Pompe disease.

At seven months, he had a tracheostomy surgery that caused him to be dependent on a ventilator machine. On October 30th, 2010, I woke up to check on my baby like I always did, just to find him not breathing and his body freezing cold. At that moment, I realized that my baby boy, after a long battle with the disease, passed away. I couldn't understand why God would take him away from me. I felt like my life was over. But God was still there.

Inspirational Affirmation

ENTRY BY: ROSEMARY HART

DAY *147*

THANKFULNESS

Your perseverance, discipline, destiny, and desire to stay focused are important. Yet nothing yields ultimate results, absent from being thankful that God is with you.

—Rosemary Hart

Inspirational Scripture

ENTRY BY: DEBORAH PERRY

DAY 148

"I beseech you therefore, brethren, by the mercies of God, that ye present your bodies a living sacrifice, holy, acceptable unto God, which is your reasonable service."

—Romans 12:1

Romans 12:1 speaks about presenting your body as being acceptable unto God, which is your reasonable service. I love this scripture because I think about how people receive us the way we present ourselves to them. I believe if we present ourselves to God as clean vessels, He can use us as clean vessels. As women, we should carry ourselves as ladies, an acceptable way unto God and others. The only way to be treated as a woman is to present yourself as a lady. God will use you the way you present yourself to Him. We have to be careful not to look at others, or the world, based on what they have. We will find ourselves becoming like the world or others who are not godly.

Preserve your mind and body.

Inspirational Quote

Entry by: Kimberly Bailey

Day *149*

A mother is the one who is still there when everyone else has deserted you.

—Author Unknown

Inspirational Quote

ENTRY BY: MIRANDA RIVERS

DAY *150*

Happiness starts with you…God's word is my happiness.

Every day I have the power to choose,
today every I choose happiness.

—MakeAVisionBoard.com

"This is the day the Lord has made; we will rejoice and be glad in it."

—Psalm 118:24

Inspirational Scripture

ENTRY BY: ESTHER BURGESS

DAY *151*

"And they shall fight against thee; but they shall not prevail against thee; for I am with thee, saith the LORD to deliver thee."

—Jeremiah 1:19

Inspirational Affirmation

ENTRY BY: JESSIE STRIGGLES

DAY *152*

The Process: Blood, Sweat, And Tears
Just Me + God = The Making of an Apostle

—Jessie Striggles

Inspirational Quote

ENTRY BY: ALICIA BAILEY

DAY *153*

Faith is taking the first step even when you don't see the whole staircase.

—Dr. Martin Luther King, Jr.

Lord, we want more faith. As I express this statement, Dr. King's quote on faith comes to my mind. Dr. King admonishes us to put on our spiritual lenses and do what the Lord has required from us. Each one of us has a legacy to fulfill. However, to accomplish the desired outcomes, there will be seasons in our lives where we must walk by faith and not by sight. Seasons in life where we must trust God as we take each step.

The Word of God states, "Because you have so little faith. Truly I tell you, if you have faith as small as a mustard seed, you can say to this mountain, 'Move from here to there,' and it will move. Nothing will be impossible for you" (Matthew 17:20 NIV). We need mountain-moving faith. It is time for us to implement the "ACT" plan: 1) Put faith into ACTION; 2) CHASE the things of God and do not look back; and 3) Be TIMELY. In other words, whatever it is that God has instructed you to achieve, do it now. Stop waiting to move based on your feelings. God is giving you permission to be free and the power to move.

There is a Walter Hawkins and Love Center Choir song titled, "When the Battle is Over." A portion of the lyrics state, "Don't wait 'till the battle is over to shout now; You know in the end, you're gonna win." I like the lyrics of the song because they support the meditation of what I believe. When you have faith, you shout in advance of the outcome. You shout in advance of the blessing. To all those reading these words, today I declare that you will begin to give God a victory praise in advance. In fact, give God an advance offering just because of who He is in your life. I am getting excited as I pen these words because God is doing a new thing in someone right now.

Prayer: I need more faith. Lord, I may not be able to see in the physical, but open my spiritual eyes and allow me to move in Your authority and Your will. God, I do not want to miss the blessings that you have set up for me. Lord, I am keeping my eyes on You. I am seeking You first because I want my God to be pleased. I love You Lord, AMEN.

Inspirational Scripture

ENTRY BY: JAE ROLLINS (JOYCE VINES)

DAY *154*

"[30]I will praise the name of God with a song, and will magnify him with thanksgiving. [31]This also shall please the LORD better than an ox or bullock that hath horns and hoofs. [32]The humble shall see this, and be glad: and your heart shall live that seek God."

— Psalm 69:30-32

Inspirational Quote

ENTRY BY: TREINNA THOMAS

DAY *155*

Don't let your emotions supersede your intelligence. Our emotions come, and then they go, your intelligence lasts a lifetime.

—Treinna Thomas

Inspirational Notes

Meet the Co-Authors

BIO: TENARIA DRUMMOND-SMITH

Tenaria Drummond-Smith, an ambitious and multi-talented entrepreneur, is the founder and visionary of Awesome Women On The Move, Inc., a personal ministry birthed in 2006 that has blossomed into a movement and an organization that promotes fellowship and unity among all women with the love of God through Jesus Christ. A native New Yorker and former civil service employee, a series of life changes motivated her to reinvent herself. She's totally souled-out as a servant of the gospel and will gladly spend her time ministering to anyone who wants to know about His grace and mercy toward her. She is a living testimony of what the power of God has done in her life and will freely tell others how He can change their lives for the better.

Tenaria has a strong passion for bringing women together from all walks of life and she emphasizes the display of love to everyone she meets. Experienced as a craft maker and event organizer, she loves giving back to the community, but the breakthrough publishing of Tenaria's first book, *I've Been Hurt In The Church*, jumpstarted her growing list of personal and professional achievements. Awesome Women On The Move has an established Facebook.com presence of 920,000+ followers (in conjunction with the Awesome Women On The Move Blog, also on Facebook), while Tenaria has a growing social media presence as a one-woman industry through Instagram, LinkedIn, and YouTube. Tenaria has the God-given vision and heart to celebrate women who do phenomenal things but are rarely recognized, and her purpose is serve as a platform to showcase women who've impacted the lives of others around them. Following her first release were two additional books co-authored with women who were willing to tell their stories of pain, inspiration, and encouragement (*Awesome Women On The Move* and *Love Grounded By Grace*). This new venture has shown Tenaria that God isn't done with her yet.

~~~
~~~

ACKNOWLEDGMENTS: JACQUELENE SCRUGGS

I want to thank God because he is the head of my life. I thank him for the Baptism in Jesus name and the precious gift of the Holy Ghost. He is my all in all.

To my loving husband, Fred L. Scruggs Sr., I want to thank you for always supporting me in everything that I do. I could not ask for a better husband. I thank God for you, and love you with all my heart.

To my loving children and grandchildren, I love you all from the bottom of my heart.

To my loving parents, the late Joe Hargrove, and Almetia Hargrove. I thank you all for raising me to be a Godly woman despite my faults. You never judged me, and for that, Mommy and Daddy, I will always love you.

Love to all my siblings and the rest of my family.

I'd like to personally thank Tenaria Drummond- Smith for always pushing me to achieve my goals. I must admit you have truly been a blessing in my life. I love you to life.

~~~

BIO: SOPHIA L. GREENE

Sophia L. Greene, a mother of six children, has spent most of her life advocating for people who think they don't have a voice or is unclear of how to use their voice to request the things they desire in life. At the age of thirteen, Sophia started using her grandmother's home as a safe haven for friends who encountered family issues. She used the pantry in the house as a mini-library to share books with her friends, who would read and share their stories while they escaped their reality and dove into the world within their minds.

Ms. Greene, being the eldest child, has spent more time in the United States than in her humble beginnings on the beautiful, troubled island of Jamaica, which she describes as a gangster paradise. After migrating to the States, Ms. Greene encountered many trials that could have taken her mind and swayed her trust from her Creator. However, she persevered through homelessness (twice), the murder of her father, and raising her children as a single mother. She refuses to allow the blows of life to make her so hard-hearted that there would be no room left to love, to extend her home or her heart to another
~~~

person's plight. Ms. Greene has worked with at-risk children for over 32 years, where she had even been led to adopt three children while raising her own. While living in an imperfect world and housed in an imperfect body, Ms. Greene's mission is to live her life being a vein of love wherever she walks. She is the author of *Ladies By The Well* and a co-author of *Love Grounded By Grace*.

~~~

BIO: THERESA BYRD

Theresa Byrd is a single parent and mother to three children and nine grandchildren. She was born in Brooklyn, New York, and is the only child of Olivia and Clad Byrd. She developed a passion for helping others in grade school, where she began lending a helping hand to teachers and friends who needed help with school work. In high school, she developed a passion for healthcare, volunteering her time at various nursing homes and hospitals. She has served as a Claims Clerk Interviewer for the National Maritime Union and a School Safety Agent for the Board of Education. Her involvement with the Board of Education inspired a passion for peer mediation and coaching. Theresa volunteered at Children Village for nine years, where she was on the Parent Counselor Board, and assisted as a visiting coach while also making a difference in the lives of children and their families.

~~~

BIO: VERA MOORE

Vera Moore, a former actress turned entrepreneur is President & CEO of Vera Moore Cosmetics. Vera was contracted on national television (NBC) as one of the first black actresses on the soap opera "Another World" where she portrayed "Linda Metcalf" for ten years and also appeared in several Broadway shows including the Tony Award-winning "Purlie Victorious." She immediately experienced the void in the market for quality products for women of color. Her mantra "SKINCARE is the TRUE foundation; makeup is an accessory. Thus, the birth of Vera Moore Cosmetics and Skincare.

Vera broke through the color barrier when her company became the first black-owned business to set up shop in the 50-year history at the prestigious Green Acres Mall Valley Stream, Long Island NY. Vera's career over the years has spanned several tv/radio shows (Dr. Oz, Sandra Bookman, Ch 7, Here N Now, Profiles with Mickey Burns, Arise), has been featured in multiple print publications (People Magazine, Allure, WWD, Black Enterprise, Crains, Network Journal's 25 Influential Black Women in Business, Beauty Store Business, Profiles with Mickey Burns, Essence), and has also appeared on the Essence Festival's entrepreneur panel.

Vera was featured in the Wall Street Journal with the announcement of her partnership with Duane Reade/Walgreens in their upscale high-end environment called the "LOOK Boutique". Vera continues to reach for "moore" with an infomercial introducing her new Skincare Signature Collection, "As Seen on TV" with original Shark Tank panel member Kevin Harrington, and the Vera Moore Cosmetics live billboard in Times Square.

Get ready as Vera comes full circle with "The Vera Moore Show." Visit us at veramoorecosmetics.com.

~~~

BIO: LESLIE DUROSEAU

Rev. Dr. Leslie Duroseau is an ordained Elder of the United Methodist church and has served as the pastor of Hamptons United Methodist Church (formerly known as Southampton UMC) located in Southampton, NY, for over 7 years. She is a sacred arts minister of dance, with more than 25 years of experience as a liturgical dance director and she is also a certified Holistic Health Counselor, training under renowned holistic health teacher, Queen Afua and graduating from the Institute of Integrative Nutrition. She is a certified holistic drugless practitioner.

Rev. Duroseau received her Doctorate of Ministry degree (D.Min) in May 2012, and her Masters of Divinity degree (M.Div) in 2008 receiving both from the prestigious New York Theological Seminary in New York. Rev. Dr. Duroseau is a certified chaplain and pastoral care counselor, certified by the College of Pastoral Care and Psychotherapy (CPSP).

Dr. Duroseau has facilitated and participated in retreats, conferences, and workshops throughout the NY area and abroad teaching sacred dance and holistic health as a methodology to fully
~~~

live out what it means and what it takes for one to be a disciple of Christ.

Most importantly, she would have all to know she loves the Lord, serves God with her whole heart, and her desire is to share the joy, compassion, and love of the Lord with everyone she encounters.

She is married to Mr. Eddy Duroseau, and they have four gorgeous children: Jasmine, Andre, Jah-le, and Jadah and two beautiful granddaughters Aiyanna and Alyssa, and my daughter-in-love Candice Spears.

~~~

BIO: LINDA M. JOHNSON

Linda earned her Master of Fine Arts degree in Creative Writing with honors from the College of New Rochelle in 2019. She is a graduate of The Christian Bible Institute Seminary (CBIS) where she earned her Associates Degree in 2019, as well as her Certificate in Biblical Studies in 2015 as the salutatorian of her graduating class. She also received her Bachelors of Arts in 2002 from The College of New Rochelle and graduated with Honors. She majored in communications and minored in broadcast journalism. She currently holds a full-time position as a professional executive assistant of a major financial institution in New York City and has over 30 years of experience.

She is a co-author of the book entitled, *Love Grounded by Grace* (by Tenaria Drummond-Smith) and is also working on her debut book to release in the summer of 2019. She is the daughter of the author, evangelist Anne Gaynelle Johnson who wrote the book *"Tear of a Man"* and *"Let The Healing Begin"*. Her mother has also produced her own CD, and many stage plays that Linda has directed. She is a deaconess married to Minister Thomas Wesley Johnson, IV, CFO of RJC Productions. Linda is the proud step-mother of five children and has six grandchildren. She and her husband currently attend church at the Powerhouse St. Luke C.O.G.I.C under the leadership of Pastor Sanford L. Henderson and Lady Sharon Henderson in the Bronx, New York.

~~~

BIO: DAWN M. COLES

Dawn M. Coles was raised in Jamaica Queens, New York. She is a compassionate and loving woman of God. At the age of sixteen, she felt God's calling on her life, which led to a deeper and more intimate relationship with Him. Dawn's love for family and community with the understanding that we are the hands and feet of Jesus who has led her into a career in Maternal/ Child Nursing as a registered nurse for over 30 years.

She has been married to her high school sweetheart Lawrence Coles, Jr. for over forty years with three adult children Lawrence III (wife Vinnessa), India, and Paul (wife Natasha). Dawn and Lawrence are the Senior Pastors of New Lyfe International Ministries a thriving church in Jamaica, Queens, New York and also serves as a Chaplain in the New York State Chaplain Task Force.

Dawn is a true example of a virtuous woman —a blessing in the home, work, and wherever God has her to be. Her greatest attribute is the heart of God that flows in her, which is manifested through her lifestyle. On any afternoon, you can find her with three beautiful precious grandchildren (Paul, Eliana, Aria), baking sweet treats or going on an amazing adventure.

~~~

BIO: KENDRA RENEE' MANIGAULT

Kendra is the founder of Greater Kingdom Fellowship of Churches and Ministries, visionary of Seniors Not 4gotten (in honor of her grandparents), Teens in Christ Teens of Change, Parents Ministry Support, Support A Sista (empowering woman entrepreneurs), the Director & Community Pastor of GO!! (Godian Operation of Outreach & Community Awareness, which serves the metropolitan area with food and clothing), 1Flesh Marriage Ministry (co-founded with Bishop Kenneth Manigault), the founder of both KRMM (Kendra Renee Manigault Ministries) and her female clergy apparel company "Pretty Preacher."

Her other accomplishments include seventeen years of service to TIAA-CREF, while also earning a Bachelor of Arts degree in Christian Counseling. She previously sat on the Queens Chapter Executive Board of Directors of the Latin African American Chaplain Association as the Executive Director of Ethics and Discipline. In 2008,
~~~

Kendra graduated from the Civilian Police Academy, where she is also a chaplain. Furthermore, she received an Honorary Doctorate of Humanitarian Service and various other recognitions and awards.

Kendra is the proud wife of Bishop Kenneth A. Manigault. They are the loving parents of their blended family of six children (Le'ja, D'Ann, Kenneth Jr., Marquis, Denzel, Tiara). Most importantly, she wants to be known as a servant of God.

~~~

BIO: LATRICIA T. DAVIS

Pastor Latricia T. Davis was born in Jamaica, New York in a Southern Christian home. She is the mother of two biological children and the adoptive mother of two nieces and two nephews, whom she raised since birth, and a spiritual mother to many others that she has met along her life's journey. She holds a Bachelor of Arts degree in Pastoral Ministries from Nyack College, specializing in Evangelism and Church Planting.

In August 2005, Pastor Davis heeded the call of God to evangelize and preach the good news of the gospel of Jesus Christ. After completing her studies, she was ordained as an evangelist in January 2007, and later ordained to the office of Elder in July of 2012.

She is the pastor and founder of Open Arms Ministries in Hollis, New York, "The Place Where The Love Of God Abides." She believes in preaching, teaching, and worshiping the Lord in Spirit and in truth. She is truly grateful that God delivered her from substance abuse, domestic violence, single parenthood, divorce, and homelessness.

Pastor Davis has had the opportunity to preach and spread the word of God in Israel and also in the heart of South Africa during several crusades. After rendering twenty-two years of service in the criminal justice system, she continues serving as a volunteer chaplain to encourage and provide spiritual care to those who are currently incarcerated.

Pastor Davis has truly come this far by "FAITH," and her utmost heart's desire is to please God, and without 'FAITH" in HIM, she knows it's impossible, but through HIM, she knows that "ALL THINGS ARE POSSIBLE TO ALL THAT BELIEVE."

~~~

BIO: CHERRYL SIMPSON

Cherryl Simpson was born on the island of Trinidad & Tobago, and migrated to New York City in February 1971. A divorceé, she is the mother of three children (Camillia, Basil II, Akil Hylton). She attended nursing school and completed her Associate degree in Applied Science from Regents College. Cherryl also completed her Bachelor of Science degree at Kaplan University (summa cum laude), and has begun pursuing a graduate degree with South University.

A resident of Mableton, Georgia, she worked as an emergency room nurse, a hospice nurse, and served in assisted living. Having a love for inspiring and encouraging women, Cherryl is venturing into the cosmetology industry. She is learning how to be the best Cherryl that she can be, losing all religion and gaining all of who she is in Christ!

~~~

BIO: JEAN THOMPSON

Jean Thompson is a Brooklyn, New York native, born in February 1961 to a black American mother and a Dominican father. She has been an employee of the New York City Police Department for over 20 years. Jean holds a baccalaureate degree from The College of New Rochelle.

She is a single mother of three adult children (Nakiya, Tiffany, Travis), and grandmother to thirteen-year-old Dior Nehemiah Bruce. She is a devoted Christian, attending a local church in Brooklyn for over twenty years and serving on the Mother's Board. Jean wears many hats in her church; a Pastor's Aid Member, Sunday School teacher, Praise and Worship Leader, assistant secretary, and a financial assistant. She also helps to serve the less fortunate in her church community, giving them hot meals and warm clothing.

In her spare time, she enjoys such hobbies as reading, crocheting, traveling, solving puzzles, and has a passion for cooking. Jean enjoys spending lots of time with her children and her family. Jean is a very active, happy, healthy, and productive woman who has many more goals and dreams in her life to pursue.
~~~

ACKNOWLEDGMENTS: ANTOINETTE HALSEY

First and foremost, I would like to thank my Heavenly Father. I'm a single mother to three wonderful children. My oldest Aquiera, who wishes she was the only child, and my twins Devon and Donte. I pray that these scriptures will uplift you through life's journey. My personal quote is "Live Life, don't allow Life to Live you!" So often we get caught up in the cares of life that we often forget to LIVE! But glory be to God.

Declare these scriptures: "I will not die but live, and will proclaim what the LORD has done." (Psalm 118:17 NIV), and, "I am come that they might have life, and that they might have it more abundantly." (John 10:10b)

~~~

BIO: TIFFANY D. KELLY

Tiffany Kelly is "The" Health Transformation Coach, author, media personality, and speaker. She is the CEO of Tiffany D. Kelly Consulting, a company dedicated to providing services that help people and their families improve their health by learning how to eat healthier and stay fit through health and wellness workshops, retreats, corporate wellness programs, and more.

She is the author of "Lady of Power: Inspirations for the Weight-loss Journey", which includes thirty-one inspirations to motivate and encourage women on their journey to a healthy lifestyle! Tiffany's own personal journey (losing over eighty pounds, curing her high blood pressure without medications, and overcoming depression and unhealthy eating habits) naturally inspires many!

Tiffany is originally from Brooklyn, New York, but now resides in the Metro Atlanta Area. She has a Bachelor of Science degree in Business Management, and a Master of Science degree in Math Education and Educational Leadership.

She has completed coursework in advanced nutrition, is a certified fitness instructor, and has over five years of experience with group fitness and weight-loss coaching. Tiffany won the 2018 Rising In Community Excellence Award (R.I.C.E.) for Health and Wellness for her dedication to helping people adopt healthier lifestyles. She has been featured on television, radio, in magazines, and as a speaker at
~~~

conferences and retreats.

When she's not working, Tiffany enjoys spending time with family and friends, thrifting, participating at her church, fitness training, creating healthy recipes, designing custom wigs, and traveling.

~~~

BIO: NINA D. BROWN

Prophetess Nina D. Brown is called to minister the gospel of Jesus Christ to those who seek help and hope in the midst of their struggles while coping with life challenges. She serves in multiple areas of ministry. She uses her gifts and life experience to enhance the Kingdom of God, under the given ministry "Majestic Wings International Ministries," which focuses on the emotional, mental and spiritual challenges of women seeking life after loss.

She is a graduate of the Fashion Institute of Technology with a dual concentration A.A.S degree in Business & Marketing; a graduate of Nyack College with a dual concentration Bachelor of Science degree in

Psychology, Pastoral Care and Counseling, and a graduate of Drew University with a Master of Divinity degree. She is currently working on her second master's degree in Clinical Mental Health at Capella University, and concluded her study with her Ph.D. in Counselor Education and Supervision from Regents University. She is a rising entrepreneur, business consultant, licensed New York State Realtor, and mentor to men and women in both ministry and business.

Nina is the proud mother of three (sons Keenan and Kenyah, daughter Keyana) and grandmother of one (Neveah Desiree). She is also a spiritual mother and mentor to many others, pushing them towards hearing the Lord say to them, "Job well done my good and faithful servant".

~~~

BIO: KEEVA DEDEWO

Keeva Dedewo is a New York City native and resident, living in Harlem with her husband and son. She came to know Christ as a young child and has since been a longstanding member of Beulah

Baptist Church, where she currently serves as a youth advisor and praise dancer.

Keeva is a retail business management professional and has worked as a Buyer/Merchandiser for leading retailers such as Target Corporation and Amazon. She earned a Master of Business Administration (MBA) degree from the Wharton School of Business at the University of Pennsylvania, and a Bachelor of Science degree from Northwestern University. Keeva has always enjoyed writing and expression. She spent her high school years serving as managing editor of her school's literary magazine and volunteering at writing workshops with local elementary school children.

Keeva is a passionate foodie and an avid traveler who has enjoyed numerous travel experiences. Her favorite travels include teaching writing to Native American children on a reservation in Montana, practicing her Spanish conversation at the University of Salamanca in Spain, performing consulting work for luxury companies in Milan, Italy and honeymooning with her husband in the islands of French Polynesia. When she is not learning her grandmother's time-tested recipes or exploring new dining experiences, she is planning new places to travel with her family.

~~~

BIO: DAWN GRANTHAM

Dawn is the wife of Henry Grantham, and mother to their two sons, Travis and Tylil Grantham. She has one daughter-in-law, Tiffany (Travis). She is also a grandmother, daughter, sister, aunt, friend, and so much more. As she has gotten older, she has learned to appreciate quality time with loved ones and not take life for granted. She enjoys socializing, networking, having fun, and mainly praising God! She is so thankful for her family and has a special love for her first grandson, Taiden Grantham.

Since 1994, Dawn has worked in advertising at various agencies, and in August 2019, she will celebrate her 11-year anniversary as a Media Reconciliation Specialist. She is currently enrolled in Ashworth University and is working towards completing her associate degree. Despite her busy schedule, she's also a faithful member at her church, serving on the trustee board and the Praise and Worship team. Because of her love for inspiring women of all ages, Dawn was the recipient of an 2018 Awesome Women On The
~~~

Move Extraordinary Woman Award for "Inspiring Others."

You can follow her on Instagram as "DGInspires", a tag that was inspired by other women approaching her with their daily life situations. She has the ability to apply biblical truth to any issue, and she is blessed to give them exactly what they need at the moment, whether it be through inspiring words, a prayer, a listening ear, or a hug. Throughout the years, Dawn has inspired women of all ages to "Live, Laugh, Love and Do it God's way!" She had hosted several successful events and inspired women at gatherings, churches, shelters, jobs, and social media. When she has spare time, you can find her supporting family, friends, crocheting, gardening, and doing arts and crafts.

~~~

BIO: ROBERTA JONES-JOHNSON

Roberta Jones-Johnson currently resides in Charlotte, North Carolina with her husband, Jerome, and son. She is a former teacher and Assistant Principal. She has a Bachelor of Science degree in Special Education, and a Master of Science degree in Education Administration and Supervision from Baruch College (CUNY), while also earning a Master of Science degree in Teaching Reading from Queens College (CUNY). She retired from the New York City Department of Education after serving students, parents, teachers, and principals for more than thirty-two years.

She has a heart for supporting and helping those she comes in contact with. She and her husband are members of Christ Pentecostal Temple (Suffragan Bishop Derrick Farmer) in Jamaica, New York. May the words of this journal give you a fresh anointing each day.

~~~

BIO: BERNETTA GREEN

A native of Norfolk, Virginia and a proud mother of three sons and one daughter, Bernetta Green has not been a stranger to life's triumphs and challenges. Bernetta dedicates her life as a stewardess to allow her tests to be a testimony of God's unfailing grace. Bernetta loves the arts in all facets. She is a loving member of Christ Pentecostal

Church in Jamaica Queens, the Phenomenal Women Empowerment Alliance of New York, a licensed New York State Realtor, and one who's honored to be a part of the Awesome Women On the Move movement.

Bernetta Green can be reached via:
E-mail: marquitez@yahoo.com
Facebook: Bernetta Green
Instagram: Berniezblog

~~~

BIO: DEBRA D. CARTER

Debra D. Carter, HHC is a Board-Certified Holistic Health Counselor, a yoga teacher, Reiki practitioner, and co-founder of Phenomenal Women Empowerment Connections, an organization of women from diverse backgrounds. The women bring their beauty, knowledge, and wisdom to uplift, encourage, inspire and empower women to discover the essence of who they are.

~~~

BIO: KAREN M. CARTER

Karen M. Carter, MS, HHC is a Board-Certified Holistic Health Counselor, nutrition coach, yoga teacher, Social Wellness Advocate, and co-founder of Phenomenal Women Empowerment Connections, a social networking organization for women that encourages positive connections and awareness to non-profit organizations that help and uplift women, children, and young adults.

As a native Long Islander (NY), Karen enjoys being out in nature walking beaches, lakes, and parks. She enjoys travel, reading inspirational books, quality time with family and friends, conducts health and wellness educational workshops, as well as teaching others how to lead a happier, healthier lifestyle.

Kmcyoga85@gmail.com
Kcholistichealth.com
Phenomenalwomenconnect.com

BIO: SHERELL FERRER

Sherell Nicole Ferrer is the founder of D.O.P.E. ("Daughters of Purpose Engaging"). The insightful, motivational speaker and teacher delights in seeing women of all ages, regardless of their challenges, living purposefully.

A native of Bronx, New York, and a devoted laborer of the Gospel, Sherell accepted her call to serve in God's vineyard at age seventeen. Taking this bold step, Sherell has remained a fervent Christian and has served in various pivotal parts of the ministry. In the course of her service in ministry, she discovered her one true purpose here on Earth— challenging women to reach their God-given potential. Through God's divine guidance, Sherell has successfully transformed the lives of numerous women by helping them draw them closer to God. She has also inspired the Pursuit of Purity movement, which teaches young women to know their value and worth.

A virtuous woman, Sherell desires not only to be an example to these women, but also be an embodiment of vitality. Sherell's greatest accomplishment is her marriage to an anointed man of God, Elder Robert Ferrer Sr., and being a proud mother of eight children.

~~~

BIO: ROSEMARY HART

Rosemary Hart is a native of Long Island, New York. She is the founder and chief architect of the Women's Center for Personal Development (WCPD). Her destiny and passion are to help women in need who demonstrate a personal commitment to growing and improving their lives by maximizing all avenues, including the progressive programming offered through the WCPD.

Rosemary has a dual responsibility as an executive administrator of Congregation of Ohav Sholom of Merrick, New York. She has held similar positions of trust at the Ahavath Achim Synagogue, of Atlanta, Georgia, where she matriculated at Georgia State University.

Rosemary is a proactive business leader with a keen ability to build and maintain crucial working relationships with stakeholders, a plethora of organizations, volunteers and like-minded business influencers.
~~~

When Rosemary is not serving the WCPD or the Congregation, she volunteers with Christian Chaplains of America, and spends treasured time with family and friends.

~~~

BIO: DEBORAH PERRY

Deborah Perry is the Assistant Pastor at Covenant Church Cathedral of Hope and Healing under the leadership of Bishop S.C.Z. Dowtin. Pastor Perry is overseer of the Women's Auxiliary, where she gives God all the praise for being a help to church members. She was born and raised in Brooklyn New York, where she still resides and serves her community as an entrepreneur.

Pastor Perry is most proud of being a child of the King. She was married to Deacon Tyrone Perry for twenty-six years until God called him to his heavenly home. She is the proud mother of two children, son Tyrone Perry Jr., and daughter Sarah Farquhar.

~~~

BIO: KIMBERLY BAILEY

Kimberly Bailey is a working wife and proud mother of a beautiful 8-year-old daughter. Kimberly is very passionate about her family, and nothing is more important to her than family. Kimberly is a self-taught baker with a budding business. It has been a long time coming, but she believes it does not matter how long it takes to reach personal success if you continue to strive. Owning her own bakery business was always one of her dreams. The other was to have a family of her own, but her journey to motherhood wasn't easy.

When Kimberly first became pregnant at age thirty-five years, she was overjoyed, but her joy would soon turn into sorrow. In the second trimester, Kimberly started feeling small contractions. Eventually, she was rushed to the hospital in active labor, but that child was miscarried. Two weeks later, her mother suffered a massive stroke and passed away exactly eight months to the date of Kimberly's miscarriage. Kimberly was at her lowest point in life. Not knowing if she could survive such devasting losses, she began to pray and seek counseling. Kimberly started to feel better, one day at a time, and that became her new approach to life —to take life one day at a time. She started to live her life to the fullest, one day at a time, keeping her faith.

Kimberly's dream was finally realized. On November 27, 2010, she gave birth via emergency C-section to a beautiful, healthy baby girl. Her daughter gave her a renewed sense of faith, then and now. Kimberly hopes that by sharing her story, she can provide inspiration and faith to those around her and beyond.

~~~

BIO: MIRANDA RIVERS

Miranda Rivers currently resides in Rosedale, NY. She received her Master degree in Adult Education from Fordham University (NY). She received her Bachelor of Arts degree in Human Services from Audrey Cohen College (New York). She volunteers in a program called WIN (Women In Need), and she loves inspiring and motivating women.

Miranda is a Nana to four beautiful grandchildren, and wife of twenty-three years to a wonderful man, Lawrence Rivers. She is recently retired after working twenty-two years in finance. She loves to travel, and one of her retirement goals is to travel to three different states and/or countries a year. Miranda uses aqua aerobics as part of her meditation.

~~~

BIO: ESTHER BURGESS

Esther Burgess is a minister who, led by the Spirit of God, has recently begun a prayer line. She has been a registered nurse since 2005. She's a wife, a mother of four children, and a stepmother of five children. Esther returned back to school to pursue a graduate degree in nursing. Prior to this, the Lord redirected her back to Bible school to pursue a doctoral degree in theology, and she's enjoying the journey. While serving in her profession, she has found God's grace to be sufficient. Esther is able to express the love of God to her patients and see the hand of God move in the lives of others.

~~~
~~~

BIO: JESSIE STRIGGLES

Apostle Jessie Striggles was born Jessie Mae Lighty in Hartsville, S.C. on December 14, 1946. She is the third child of ten children born to Janie Mae Lighty and Jess Lighty. Jessie's joy for being the first member of her family to graduate from high school was cut short with the tragic loss of her mother in a car accident, just two days after Jessie's graduation. Depending on her father to take care her and her siblings after losing their mother, Jessie experienced another tragedy two years later when he died.

Jessie met and married a wonderful and generous man, Cardell Striggles II, who was her strength and support during this time. She is a mother to two sons, Cardell Striggles III, and Justin Striggles. Apostle Striggles shared an incredible 14 years of marriage with her beloved husband; only to lose him in a tragic car accident in 1979. She surely thought this loss would take her out of the picture, had it not been for her two sons giving her a reason to live. As a single mother, life wasn't easy for Jessie, but God equipped her, gave her the favor of men, and gave her the strength to minister to so many people across the country.

~~~

BIO: ALICIA BAILEY

Rev. Alicia Bailey is a bi-vocational professional. She is the pastor of St. John's African Methodist Episcopal (AME) Church in Brooklyn, New York. She is also the Assistant Director of Benefits Services in the Human Resources department at NYU Langone Health Center (NYC).

Rev. Alicia holds a Master of Divinity degree and a Certificate in Christian Ministry from New York Theological Seminary, a Bachelor's Degree in Business Administration from Pace University, and she has completed all requirements necessary to be ordained AME Itinerant Elder. She is a teacher in the New York Conference AME Ministerial Institute, while also serving as the NY Conference Women In Ministry (WIM) Coordinator. Prior to her appointment to St. John AME Church, Rev. Bailey served as the Pastor of James/St. Philip AME Church from June 2010 to June 13, 2015.

She has organized and coordinated seminars, retreats, conferences, orientations, and business meetings. She is one of the
~~~

contributing authors of a book titled "How to Survive When Your Ship is Sinking." She has been the recipient of many awards such as "Minister of the Year" by the Williamsbridge Club of the National Association of Negro Business and Professional Women's Club.

Rev. Alicia is the daughter of Veronica Morris and the late Clayton Nesmith. She has one sister, Tahitia, and one brother, Eric. She is married to her soulmate, Randall Bailey, and they have one daughter, Adrianna Alicia Bailey. Rev. Alicia enjoys the company of her family members and friends, traveling, listening to music, rapping, comedy shows/films, empowering people, and telling jokes. Her favorite scripture is Proverbs 3:5-6 ("Trust in the LORD with all thine heart; and lean not unto thine own understanding. In all thy ways acknowledge him, and he shall direct thy paths").

~~~

BIO: JAE (JOYCE) ROLLINS

Joyce Rollins (affectionately known as Jae) was born in Brooklyn, NY, on July 13, 1969. Coming from humble beginnings as a child of a single working mother, she studied hard to make her mother proud. Jae studied at Medgar Evers College and Empire State College, where she majored in Business Management. Jae has worked in the advertising industry for the past thirteen years.

Chasing after her first love, music, Jae has had the privilege of traveling the world under the leadership of Bishop Hezekiah Walker. Through his ministry, she sang background for Grammy award-winning artists and many mainstream audiences. Jae is married to Teddie "FX" Rollins, a musical genius in his own right. She serves diligently at her church, always lending a hand where one is needed.

No matter where she wound up, she always found herself on the road singing or chasing her second love, baking. Jae attended Star Academy, and in July 2016, she opened her home-based baking business, Centerpiece Cakez ("At the heart of everything sweet is the centerpiece"). Jae offers her clients whimsical, custom designs that fit the theme of the celebration.

Most recently Zhaki2 Entertainment and Events ("Executed with Excellence") was established when Jae saw the need to upgrade standards in the hospitality events industry. A new passion for living well was birthed, and as a Wellness Ambassador, it is her goal to help
~~~

ignite the desire for God's people to live well.

Jae is many things: a mother to four children (Xavier-Jamaal, Kai-Sakile, Kayla, Keyaira), a daughter, a wife, and grandmother, but one thing that everyone should know about her is that she's a child of God, a glory carrier!

~~~

BIO: TREINNA THOMAS

Treinna is a Licensed Master Social Worker (LMSW) at the Office of Mental Health within the Department of Corrections (NYS). Her passion for social work has been a part of her from a young age.

In the field of social work, she has had the opportunity to learn so much about herself, while striving to be a pillar of hope for those who may be struggling with their mental health and other life challenges. Treinna knows first-hand about dealing with life challenges, having faced a diagnosis of pancreatic cancer, the risk of losing her home, and currently facing a challenge with a fibromyalgia diagnosis.

Treinna also knows first-hand about what an awesome God she serves and whom she strives to live for according to His word. She takes pride in herself, her efforts, and her passion. Her belief is that with support, a listening ear, a heap of faith, empathy, compassion, and determination, people can change and make progress to succeed.

~~~

www.ingramcontent.com/pod-product-compliance
Lightning Source LLC
Chambersburg PA
CBHW070950180726
48291CB00004B/1235

* 9 7 8 1 9 4 2 8 7 1 6 7 5 *